Open Mind Zen
A Guide to Meditation

by Al Rapaport
edited by Sydney Rapaport

ISBN: 978-1-60402-307-7

Library of Congress Control Number: 2003095192

Open Mind Zen Press

www.OpenMindZen.com

Contents

As the speed and complexity of modern life increases, meditation can serve as a powerful antidote to stress, lack of direction and miscommunication. What one can reasonably expect from developing a personal meditation practice.

How all systems of meditation ever developed break down into three basic styles. Advantages and disadvantages of each one.

An analysis of what thinking really is, how to deal with it, and how it is often misunderstood as it relates to meditation practice.

The Western model of id, ego and superego as it relates to the Buddhist concept of the elimination of ego through meditation. This is not as scholarly as it sounds!

A discussion of the importance of being a beginner in all things.

Everyone hates being a beginner, but there just isn't anywhere else to start! Problems that plague beginning and experienced meditators.

IV

Foreword

All human beings have a deep need to look within for the answers to life's mysteries, and the methods of doing so have remained virtually unchanged for thousands of years. However, the language and style of teaching that was appropriate in ancient India or China may not be appropriate to reach you, the reader. This book was written to transmit the heart of meditation teaching in a way that virtually anyone today can understand, with the sincere belief that it is essential to respect the ancient traditions, but at the same time not be attached to them.

Zen Meditation, which was introduced to the West a scant 40 years ago, is part of a 2600-year-old tradition which migrated from India and Nepal (where the historical Gautama Buddha lived and taught) through Tibet, China, Japan and eventually the United States and Europe. Zen is unlike any other form of meditation in certain ways, and its paradoxical presentation, which captured the minds of beatnik poets and intellectuals in the 1960's, continues to fascinate many today. Zen is not a technique, per se, but rather is a way of freeing ourselves from the constraints of our own self-imposed limitations. In the following pages we will be discussing this unique system of meditation, and as we do we will be helping to define a truly American expression of this ancient spiritual practice.

In writing *Open Mind Zen*, there were three primary purposes guiding me:

1) To develop a book on Zen that any beginner can pick up and understand without extensive knowledge of Buddhist terminology or dogma;

2) That this book should also be substantial enough to interest those who have been meditating for a number of years;

3) That the book should be oriented towards the layperson practicing partly or mostly on their own, as most practitioners

are in the West.

The teaching I've done over the years has convinced me that there is a tremendous desire on the part of many people to learn meditation. However, the Asian models of the past often don't reach modern Westerners. *Open Mind Zen* addresses this need for information and puts it in the hands of those who would most benefit from it. It is a book that beginning Zen meditators can learn from, and advanced meditators can enjoy and give to family or friends that ask how to meditate.

My sincere desire is to help in some small way to contribute to the awakening of the planet. My teachers have been extremely generous in what they've given – not holding anything back. I hope in some small way I've done the same in this book.

Chapter 1

Why Meditate?

When an individual has direct experience of the fact that he or she is one with others and indeed with the entire universe, a host of ills dissipate on their own without direct, conscious intervention of any sort.

Al Rapaport

Ever hear the expression, "If you have to ask the price, you can't afford it?" In a sense, if we need to ask the question, "why meditate?" we are not yet ready to begin the journey. Chances are, if you are reading this page you already have some attraction to or desire to meditate. Those who wish to learn meditation seem to have some type of feeling, no matter how vague, that looking within can provide the answer to the mysteries of life and death, as well as what to do in between.

Of course, meditation can bring many benefits, including better health, increased ability to concentrate, stress reduction and the like. But ultimately what Zen is about is the quest for enlightenment, or the gaining of true understanding about what it means to be a human being. When an individual has direct experience of the fact that he or she is one with others and indeed with the entire universe, a host of ills dissipate on their own without direct, conscious intervention of any sort. The experience of enlightenment, which has been a part of all esoteric religious traditions for thousands of years, is truly the one real answer to the question, "Why meditate?" The main point in Zen teaching is that we must make this experience our own, that we must experience it in the very marrow of our bones! One thing is for sure – we can't learn about meditation by talking or reading about it. We can get a good intellectual foundation this way, but to really learn about meditation we must simply do it. In this way, meditation practice is similar to virtually any other human endeavor. For instance, we can read a thousand books on swimming and still drown in deep water. All our intellectual knowledge in that case wouldn't do us any good, as the knowledge of swimming must be ingrained in our body and mind in order to save ourselves from drowning. When learning to play a musical instrument, we can't just read about how to do it, but must spend time practicing with our body. Likewise, we must commit our minds *and* bodies to our meditation in order to experience its true effects.

3

As we progress along our meditation path, we find that our life changes radically. Although the effects vary somewhat from person to person, inevitably most find that they are much better able to observe the difficulties in their lives rather than being brought down by them. Watching the mind in meditation, the rising and falling away of thought, feeling and emotion, gives us an internal strength which we can apply to any life endeavor. Many find that their creativity increases as they link up with the true source of all creativity, the *unborn mind*, and that their concentration is much stronger.

But inevitably, what meditation is about is being able to face life and death with understanding and a clear conscience. Learning to let go of past and live in the present moment is the invaluable lesson of Zen practice.

Chapter 2

Types of Meditation

It is clear, even in an intellectual sense, that neither the past nor the future actually exist, except in thought. It is scientifically impossible to be anywhere but in the moment, but somehow we don't feel as if we are. From the very beginning we are already totally present and fully enlightened, but just don't realize it.

Al Rapaport

Throughout human history many forms of meditation have been developed, and yet all deal with the same basic issue: the problem of the human mind and how to become free. In investigating many meditation systems, it seems there are three basic ways of categorizing their techniques. These 3 categories are: concentration, awareness and just being. Of course, awareness has a component of concentration, and just being has a component of awareness, etc. The following information is meant to help clarify the bewildering number of methods now available to the modern-day seeker.

Concentration

All of us face the problem of how to quiet the mind when we sit down to meditate, or when we attempt to do anything in a focused manner. We often feel that our mind is out of control or that we cannot quite bring things into focus, and as a result most forms of meditation are the concentration type. Now if we examine the word, *concentration*, it normally means to condense or narrow – focusing on one thing to the exclusion of all others. So essentially what is happening in all concentration type exercises is we are trying to take the mind or the attention and narrow the focus, thereby excluding distracting thoughts. Ultimately, concentration forms of meditation are designed to narrow our focus to such an extent that we are able to concentrate on one thing only. We eventually reach a point in concentration where we are able to keep one thing in front of us exclusively during our meditation. Although this is not the end goal of meditation, it is always a major step, and can take years to accomplish.

There are numerous systems of meditation that employ the technique of concentration, including mantra, TM, visualizations, and in Zen, beginning koan practice (see chapter 15 for more on *koans*). Any type of meditation where we are focusing on one specific thing to the exclusion of other things and using our force of will and energy to achieve that purpose or goal could be in this category. Some visualization techniques use this method also, such as envisioning a flower or a pleasant scene.

Naturally, there are advantages and disadvantages to any form of meditation, so we must find out by trial and error which is best for our particular nature. When we find a good method, it is important to stick with it and not hop around too much from practice to practice. So, the weakness of the concentration form of practice is that it is very difficult to devote ourself exclusively to concentration for any amount of time in this culture and with the life-style that most of us have. The strength of this form of practice is that we tend to get rapid results. Concentration forms of meditation work best in a kind of lifestyle where we are living in a very segregated environment like a monastery or meditation center. For the most part, in those situations things are being taken care of for us and there is a set schedule that encourages us to drop our everyday lives and just do the practice. If we devote ourselves totally to a concentration practice it can have very powerful results very quickly. However, it is very difficult for most beginning meditators to progress with concentration unless they are in the proper environment, and the unfortunate result of over-adherence to concentration is often frustration, leading to discontinuation of meditation altogether.

Awareness

In awareness forms of meditation, rather than creating something that is not already happening we simply become aware of something that is actually happening. For instance, all of us at this very moment are either involved in an inhale or an exhale. Even in deepest sleep we are involved in inhaling or exhaling – we are breathing all the time we are alive. So, in breath awareness meditation we are simply being aware of something that is already occurring in a given moment. In awareness practice we may be observing something we are doing, such as breathing, that we are not normally conscious of, or it may be something such as just listening to sounds around us.

What we start to find when we do this type of exercise is how much of the time our attention is not focused on what is actually happening in a given moment, but rather in our thinking, fantasizing, and projecting. The mind is always going, going, going! This becomes painfully obvious to beginners – all of a sudden we realize how little control we have. It can be very disconcerting, and it keeps many people from continuing to practice. But the fact is that we have to start somewhere, so if we really see this problem and want to do something about it, we have to take the bull by the horns and deal with the difficulty. As we gain more experience, things get better, just as when we are learning to play a musical instrument we sound terrible at first, but after a few years of practice it goes more smoothly. After awhile we don't have to think about the instrument at all, we just do it. It's the same with meditation.

Awareness meditation is often the best method for most people to begin with. It is used extensively in many schools of Zen and other forms of Buddhist meditation. Undoubtedly the best-known way of doing this form of meditation is what is called *watching the breath*, or breath awareness, as was previously mentioned. In this practice, when we are sitting and involved in the meditation process we actually turn our attention inward with our eyes closed and observe the rising and falling of the breath. It's truly amazing how powerful this practice is! It sounds very simple, but when we do it for a length of time we find that our mind keeps getting off track. At a deeper level:

> *When we inhale, the air comes into the inner world.*
>
> *When we exhale, the air goes out to the outer world.*
>
> *The inner world is limitless, and the outer world is also limitless.*
>
> *We say "inner world" or "outer world", but actually there is just one whole world.*

In this limitless world, our throat is like a swinging door,

The air comes in and goes out like someone passing through a swinging door...

What we call "I" is just a swinging door which moves when we inhale and when we exhale.

—Zen Mind, Beginner's Mind

by Shunryu Suzuki, Page 29

Keep in mind that the first few months of meditation practice are like trying to tame a bucking bronco! In the beginning we are off the horse a lot more than we are in the saddle! This is definitely not a learn-in-one-weekend method, but rather takes years to develop. We actually never stop learning and refining our awareness, and after ten or fifteen years there is still more to learn and deeper levels to go. It is an infinite process. This is what is called *beginner's mind* – realizing that we are always able to learn more and we are always beginning every time we sit down to meditate.

Now, back to awareness meditation in general. Anything we are observing with any of our senses could be an awareness meditation provided we are using it as such. One woman I spoke with was relating how she used to work in a fish cannery somewhere up in Maine. She said that when she started out she got bored very quickly, as each person standing at the conveyer belt did just one task to each fish moving by. All day long, all she did was cut the heads off fish, one after the other. But after awhile, she was able to treat this as a meditation, and realized that there was an opportunity through the repetition to increase awareness. This realization totally changed the experience for her, and the previously boring job became a meditation rather than a chore.

Another extremely effective form of meditation is simply being aware of sensations arising in the body/mind while sitting still and turning the attention inward. In other words, whatever sensations arise during the meditation process, just notice them. You may feel tension, fluttering, openness, etc. The object here is rather than being involved in the conceptual aspect, such as "I am nervous," get down to its most basic level, such as what does "I am nervous" feel like, what is the actual physical sensation associated with that concept. Allow your breath and awareness to sink in your body so it falls out of your head and neck area and more into the lower abdominal area. From this perspective, just notice the arising and falling away of the various sensations. There is no right or wrong way to do it, just simply observe. If your thinking is too powerful, just notice the physical sensations associated with rapid thinking.

Anyone can do this, and at virtually any time: walking down the street, riding in a bus, or sweeping the front porch. The object here is to *experience* the sensations, not just think about them! Some practitioners have a very difficult time of this, as they are not used to simply feeling what is going on internally and have a tendency to constantly intellectualize. This type of practice can certainly be done in a monastery or meditation center, but is also wonderful for those with everyday jobs and relationships. Since the object is simply to notice what is happening, whatever sensation is arising *is* the meditation. This eliminates the tendency to judge ourself, as often happens during concentration forms of meditation when we cannot effectively concentrate because of an overactive mind.

Just Being

This is probably the hardest form of meditation to convey to the beginner. Since it is incredibly simple it is the most advanced technique. Normally, when we attend school, the more advanced we get the more complex the information is but in meditation the simpler techniques are the most advanced. In Japanese, this form

11

of practice is called *Shikan Taza*, or just sitting. The Tibetans call it *Dzog Chen*. It involves simply being present with no technique, no special concentration or awareness.

Sometimes, during a quick, painful episode such as stubbing our toe, for an instant there is no perception of what has actually happened. It has taken us so much by surprise that in that instant we are experiencing the stimulus of the toe hitting something without any labels or distinctions. At that time there is usually no pain, but the thoughts that arise immediately following the incident bring with them pain, recrimination, anger and other forms of suffering. This illustrates the difference between just being (the experience of the initial instant) and the conceptualization that occurs after that. This is true of all sensory experience, and relates to the fact that all experience when it first occurs is a pure or universal experience. Then, somehow we take that experience and add our conditioning to it. A short time period after the initial experience occurs, all our concepts about it come up: saying it was good or bad, describing it and then reacting to it in response to our particular conditioning. To meditate effectively, we must begin to understand how we take present, universal experience and turn it into a relative concept.

It is clear, even in an intellectual sense, that neither the past nor the future actually exist, except in thought. It is scientifically impossible to be anywhere but in the moment, but somehow we don't feel as if we are. From the very beginning we are already totally present and fully enlightened, but just don't realize it. To illustrate this point, say you are poverty stricken and just scrape together enough money to move into an old house. The former resident was an old miser who had stashed millions in gold under the floorboards, but when he died, the knowledge of the location of the gold died with him. You could be living on top of enough money to feed and clothe you for life, but if you don't know it's there, you can starve to death in your ignorance!

Until you know the gold is there and can get to it, you aren't going to be able to make use of its buying power. So, you have to be aware that enlightenment is your birthright before you can begin to claim it for your own and make use of it. This is a very important point that we should be aware of from the beginning, that enlightenment is not far away, but is with us all the time. Having faith in this fact serves as a form of positive reinforcement that begins to pervade our entire life.

The key to being is *to be one with*. So, ideally when we are meditating we are one with the breath; when we are listening we are one with hearing, when we are walking we are one with walking, and so on. But because our conditioning runs so deep, this very simple activity can be difficult to achieve until one has been practicing awhile.

Al Rapaport

Chapter 3

I Think, Therefore I am Not

Trying to stop thoughts is a bit like trying to hold a beach ball under water. The very nature of the air inside the ball is lighter than the water, so the ball wants to come up to the surface. You can keep the ball submerged, but it takes constant energy to do so.

Al Rapaport

We used to run a listing in a local holistic directory in Western Massachusetts for our meditation group. The headline, which I had used for years was, "Zen – It's not what you think!" People who called would inevitably ask, "Well, if it's not what I think, what is it?" Obviously, whatever someone's idea about Zen is, it is just a concept. Yet each moment that the caller is living and breathing, their Zen is being manifested through everything they do. Once our mental descriptions begin to arise, we have already missed the moment, and cannot capture what Zen is. It doesn't even matter what our mental concepts are – they can be lofty and pure in nature or horrible and outlandish – all are equal in missing the point, which is moment to moment reality.

Many participants of my workshops have said, "I can't meditate because I can't stop my thoughts." Well, you don't have to stop your thoughts to meditate, and even most experienced meditators can't stop their thoughts for any length of time. The only way to eliminate thoughts is to allow them to come up and dissipate. Trying to stop thoughts is a bit like trying to hold a beach ball under water. The very nature of the air inside the ball is lighter than the water, so the ball wants to come up to the surface. You can keep the ball submerged, but it takes constant energy to do so. Thoughts, ideas and feelings we want to avoid or stop are just like the ball. Their very nature is to be expressed and then disappear, but what happens is we often hold them in. Perhaps we are afraid that we will be overpowered by the suppressed, emotional content of our thoughts and feelings – or that those around us will think us strange or not love us if we let our true feelings surface. As a result we spend tremendous energy keeping a lid on it all. Obviously, this ties up a huge amount of our vital energy in a type of conflict that is not productive in the least, and leads to stress and disease.

I was having lunch a number of years ago with famous teacher who has written several popular books on healing, meditation and the mind, and he told me a story about a woman who, during one of his workshops, said that she couldn't stop her mind from thinking all the time. Of course, this is the problem that virtually everyone has when they begin meditation, and is the source of constant irritation! So he asked her, "well, were you ever aware of that before?" She replied, "No, I was never aware of the fact that even when nothing seemed to be going on that I was thinking so much." To which he replied, "You have made a major step. You are now much more aware, but your awareness is showing you something you don't want to see." In other words, even though all she could do when she meditated was constantly think, she was now aware of the fact that her mind was constantly thinking. She wasn't comfortable with the fact that her mind was that much out of her control.

We are all like this to greater or lesser degrees when we begin the awareness process of meditation. We first sit the body down and eliminate the obvious movements of the head, neck, body arms and legs, but what we are left with is the constantly occurring but largely unconscious movement of the mind. Often people ask why they have to sit still. Somehow, sitting still creates the opportunity to be able to see what is going on in the mind most of the time: a mishmash of circular, useless thinking, or what we call *monkey mind*. If that's what you see for the first month, six months or year that you meditate, just realize that most people aren't even aware this is occurring at all.

Often, beginning meditators say, "The meditation is making me think too much," as if meditation can *make* them do anything! Somehow, people tend to blame the meditation as a way of transferring responsibility from themselves. It's easy to say the meditation is the problem, rather than admitting that one's mind is out of control.

Another thing beginning meditators often say is that they have taken off during mediation. It's important to realize that *we* don't really go anywhere during this process we're still sitting there. But the power of thinking is such that we can think we

18

are gone, when in fact we are present at all times. We can never underestimate the power of thought.

Most of us function in such an unconscious state most of the time. We are reacting to things and not aware of why we react the way we do, why our life is so confused, or why we can't concentrate. That is because our minds are largely unconscious to us. The word unconscious, basically means *not conscious of*. Through meditation we attempt to bring that which is not conscious into our conscious awareness, thereby making our whole life conscious.

In Zen the object is to experience for ourselves in a total fashion what the mind is, not just to know it intellectually. To do that, we have to experience it in the body and mind simultaneously. Normally, we think of the body being somehow separate from our mind, but the premise behind many holistic healing systems and meditation systems is to realize the oneness of body and mind. One of the primary teachings of Zen is that the body and mind are from the very beginning *already* one. Therein comes the paradox – if the body and mind are essentially one, why doesn't it feel that way? Why do the body and mind seem separate? In Zen practice you have to experience the answer to this question yourself, and to do that, normal thinking must be transcended. For instance, if you went to a country where there were no apples, and the people there had never tasted one, how would you explain to them how an apple tasted? (Let's say they did have oranges and pears.) The only way you could attempt to convey the taste would be by comparing it to something they had tasted, for instance, "it's round like an orange, firmer than a pear, a little different taste, etc." It is clear, though, that these people are going to have to bite into the apple to really know what it tastes like. At the moment that they take a bite, they will know and no more words will be necessary. It's the same thing in meditation practice. You have to experience for yourself what the mind is, what life is, what death is – all those things are tied up in the same issue,

19

that of the mind. It doesn't matter what you read or what anyone tells you, you still have to experience it for yourself.

Chapter 4

Ego and the Mind

With enough investigation through meditation, our idea of what the mind is begins to break down, and we realize that there is something else going on...

Al Rapaport

The dictionary is always a good place to start when defining a term, as it gives the society's conceptual view. The word ego is used often in Buddhist writing, as well as in Western psychological language, but the meaning can be very different. Nevertheless, it is very interesting to see what the dictionary says.

The mind is broken down in the Western psychological sense into three parts: the *id*, the superego and the ego. Those distinctions don't really exist as such in Zen philosophy. According to the dictionary, the id is that part of the psyche which is the source of instinctive energy. What is very interesting about this, is that in the dictionary definition it is meant in a negative sense; as the id being manifested in "impulses" such as cravings, desires, etc. which are controlled through the ego and the superego.

There are various definitions of the ego, but in a psychological sense it is often defined as that part of the psyche which experiences the external world through the senses and consciously controls the impulses of the id. Nothing is said about the internal world, because that world is not often recognized in Western thought. What a horrible thing to be doing, to have to be constantly, consciously controlling our deep, dark id impulses. It seems like such a chore and a burden. Of course, if we live this way, it is a burden – we constantly have to be watching out lest the devil (id) make us do something that we really don't want to do. (Hum...or do we?) Ah, those idle hands. In this particular Western psychological model, the ego is actually a part of the mind which regulates or experiences the input from the senses. But we are not told what that thing which experiences the senses actually is. On a personal, experiential level, it does not really explain what the ego is, it just says that there is something there that experiences.

But what is that? What is that self, that ego that processes and controls the sensory input? Is it an actual thing or not?

The superego is defined as that part of the psyche which

23

controls, at the *unconscious* level, the impulses of the id. Then the dictionary says a very interesting thing next, which is that the superego is the *conscience* of the unconscious. In other words, according to this psychological model the superego on an unconscious level controls the deeper, instinctual urges (The instinctive energy of the id).

There is an early 60's science fiction movie called *Forbidden Planet* in which a group of explorers visit an alien world. Eventually, they encounter a gigantic monster which was somehow created by the collective id of an ancient extinct culture. This monstrous being had destroyed the culture that had spawned it, and now threatened to do the same to the brave group of astronauts. In a way, this movie was a model for many people's concept of the human id. The idea of the id as a negative, dark, instinctive energy is tied up in a very Western concept of the self and the mind. From the Zen perspective, what we would call the most basic energy would be the *Buddha-Mind* energy, which underlies the entire universe. Zen tradition teaches that this energy is beyond positive or negative in the absolute sense, yet is the primal energy which animates everything. In other words, this energy does not have to be feared.

With enough investigation through meditation, our idea of what the mind is begins to break down, and we realize that there is something else going on than what we have previously been taught. The interesting thing about this knowledge is that it comes to us on a comprehensive body/mind level. It is very difficult for those who have not had any meditation experience to understand this point, because at first we feel both physically and psychologically that there is some thing there. As we begin to meditate, and for years afterwards, we still feel that there is some self or ego that is the watcher. This corresponds to the ego as defined above, processing information, observing, tasting, hearing, etc. But when we try through meditation to clearly understand what the ego/mind consists of, we find it is very slippery. Every time we try to catch or identify it, it slips away. As our meditation practice progresses and we are unable to define or identify the mind, our view of it becomes much less solid, and we see it more as a fluid process than a thing. Nevertheless, the tendency to make fluid processes solid dies hard – we have to constantly be aware of our tendency to do so.

Often in spiritual practice we are told to let go of the ego. Yet, if the ego is not a thing, as we have stated above, what is there to let go of? Obviously, the only thing we can let go of are our ideas and concepts. Even the dreaded concepts themselves are not real things, but rather a pattern of mind/body activity that we have allowed ourselves to fall into. So what we normally call attachment to ego is actually attachment to our concepts about it. These concepts manifest in the way we move, how we relate to others and how we live our lives in the greater sense.

Another interesting aspect of our use of the word, ego, is our expression that someone "has a big ego." Are we speaking here of an actual thing someone is carrying around? Another way of saying this in English is that someone has a "big head." This is tied up in the Western concept of the mind as being all in the head. It is obvious that a person "with a big ego" is someone who *thinks* they are really great, and because they think so much of themselves they are attempting to convey it through their body language and actions. People of this sort walk around with an attitude, which becomes what we call the ego. In Japan they would say that a person has a big hara, or big belly. (The hara is a spot slightly below the navel.) The meaning though is different, in that someone with a big hara has great personal power, charisma or energy, in a positive sense. Ego is often confused with *big hara*, which is a method of living and expressing ourselves completely without the posturing that big ego brings. The most highly realized teachers I have met in my life all had a natural, dynamic presence unburdened by attachment to ego. Unfortunately, this entire way of living is misunderstood in our present time and

25

culture, and big hara is often mistaken for big ego.

Obviously, we don't have to give up our personality in order to overcome the ego and experience enlightenment. As ego is a concept and not a real thing, it must be let go of to grow spiritually. But *personality* is how we naturally and individually manifest our true nature in our lives, and as such, does not hinder our experience of enlightenment. Every person and every thing has a unique and independent existence, and as such is absolute in and of itself. When we realize this truth we become secure and do not have to attempt to maintain an image for others. Our image is automatically projected through everything we do every minute we are alive. If we allow ourselves to just *be*, then before we *do* anything we are this amazing, unique being which doesn't require external affirmation. So, there is a tremendous difference between *just being* and *trying to be*. Just being is the natural, pristine state of pure existence. *Trying to be* is trying to add on to or create something that is already created. In Zen literature, this is called "putting a head upon your head," which as we all know results in changing ourself into a two-headed monster!

It is clear that our ego and our self-consciousness manifests through our actions in every way. When I was in Southern Europe in the early 1970's I was quite impressed with how many people, especially in the smaller towns, were out walking in the evening rather than sitting in front of a TV. Those that weren't walking were sitting on park benches watching those walking. In Spanish, there is even a word for walking around so others can see you, called *pasear*. Anyway, sitting watching people walk in a busy area, one can truly get a sense of the person's mind-state. You'll see men strutting in such a way as to emphasize their physical size and strength, beautiful women dressed to kill with their noses in the air, acting as if they don't want to be looked at, etc. On the opposite end, there are those that seem crushed by life, hunched over or with head hanging low, looking down at the ground. So, our concept of ego creates our body, in the sense that it creates the way we do things, including the way we move and the armor or tension throughout our bodies which defines the way we appear to others. The degree to which our mind effects our body is truly amazing. Years ago, during a week long meditation retreat, I was asked to speak with a woman who was complaining of stomach pain. My first question to her was to ask if the pain was happening only during the meditation, to which she replied in the affirmative. "In that case," I said, "you don't have to worry, as it is just a manifestation of ego resistance, and it will eventually disappear with no other consequences." Had it been a constant pain that didn't go away, I would have taken her to see a doctor. She took my advice and the psychosomatic discomfort disappeared later in the retreat.

Ego is often regarded as the enemy in spiritual traditions. As long as this adversarial relationship exists, the ego needs to be exhausted and beat into submission for awakening to occur. This is often accomplished by lack of sleep, long, exhausting hours of meditation, repetition and psychological and physical stress of various sorts. This process does work for those who can weather the storm, but it often takes years, and many don't make it due to the pain and frustration. It is much better to give the ego voice, yet understand that it is only a part of who we are. Then we can literally ask it to get out of the way, so that the Buddha Mind can shine through. To accomplish this, we need to recognize that the ego has an important function for the self – that of regulating and protecting. Rather than threatening its protective status, we need to enlist the ego's help in discovering that part of the mind which is beyond the ego's scope. In this way the ego becomes an ally in our practice.

Al Rapaport

Chapter 5

Beginner's Mind/ Enlightened Mind

The sign of a true adept on any spiritual path is the ability to constantly maintain beginner's mind—to be enlightened by all things – to realize that wisdom is constantly being revealed by masters, fools, babies, rocks and trees.

Al Rapaport

The word *self* is used in different ways in Zen. Self with a small 's' is usually referred to as the Western idea of ego-self and big 'S'. Self is usually what is called the Universal Self. Dogen Zenji, one of the founders of Zen in Japan, wrote a treatise called the *Shobogenzo*, which literally means the "Way of Everyday Life." In fact, Zen itself is often referred to as the Way of Everyday Life. The most quoted part of the Shobogenzo are the following lines: "To study the Way (Tao) is to study the self. To study the self is to forget the self. To forget the self is to be enlightened by all things." When we meditate, what we are doing is studying or becoming aware of the self, or how the ego manifests. The next part is a lot harder for most to understand: "To study the self is to forget the self." This is why we say that when we are practicing Zen, we aren't really *learning* anything in the intellectual sense, but rather unlearning or forgetting our notions of who we are. The third part of this, "To forget the self is to be enlightened by everything," is a way of describing the experience of enlightenment. It isn't until we forget the self or totally drop our concept of something that it is capable of enlightening us. If we can do it, we can be enlightened by anything in an instant, which is another way of saying we have gotten out of the way and are allowing that thing to enlighten us as to what it really is.

On a personal level this means that we must listen and observe in order to be enlightened by others, not halfheartedly, but with our whole being. If we enter into a relationship or experience with this attitude we can learn a tremendous amount, but if we allow our inner dialogue to interfere then no true communication can take place. I used to see examples of this in the karate dojo where I practiced and taught. When students who had studied in another system came to try out our particular style, it was difficult for some of them to let go of what they had learned before.

This is especially true of those who had previously attained some intermediate or advanced rank – their concepts of how they

31

used to do things could get in the way and prevent them from absorbing the new, pertinent teachings.

There is a famous Zen story about a student that wishes to study with a particular master. He visits the Zen master and the master pours him tea. But the master doesn't stop when the cup is full and keeps pouring and pouring until tea is running all over the table! The student, visibly shocked, asks the master what he is doing, to which he replies that just as he cannot pour more tea into a full cup, he cannot teach the student if he is full of his own ideas. It was obvious to the master that this student was too full of himself to learn anything. The moral of this story is that we must be willing to let go of our own ideas to receive teaching from others.

The sign of a true adept on any spiritual path is the ability to constantly maintain beginner's mind – to be enlightened by all things – to realize that wisdom is constantly being revealed by masters, fools, babies, rocks and trees. The degree to which we are able to go into a situation fresh and without concepts is the degree to which we will truly learn what is being imparted. Suzuki Roshi, in the very beginning of the Zen classic *Zen Mind, Beginner's Mind* says, "In the beginner's mind there are many possibilities, but in the expert's there are few." We have all seen annoying experts who are so expert that they seem incapable of hearing any other perspective. Beginners, on the other hand, realize they don't know, and so they learn a tremendous amount. Their minds are like a sponge, soaking up everything around them. The more of a beginner we can be, the more we will receive and the more we will "be enlightened by all things." It is of paramount importance to keep this attitude, whether we are a beginner or an experienced meditator. No matter how many years of meditation, we never stop going deeper, never stop being a beginner.

When we look at a flower with our whole being, empty of concepts, that flower will enlighten us as to what *flowerness* is about. If we can't let go of our concepts about the flower, this can't happen. Of course, the flower and everything else in the universe is constantly changing, so we can constantly be re-enlightened by everything around us. Isn't it wonderful? The whole universe is constantly being born and revealed. But somehow, we get so attached to our way of seeing things, to our limited perspective, that we often miss the incredible spectacle of creation happening all the time. There is a Zen koan, or question, that asks, "When was the universe created?" The point is that creation is happening as you read these words.

We can experience enlightenment through any of the senses. When we eat a meal, how much of the time are we actually experiencing the taste of the food? When monkey mind is active, we can consume an entire meal and not taste anything. Eating with a clear mind, the various tastes enlighten us as to their nature – we don't know exactly what the taste will be before we experience it.

In fact, enlightenment always occurs through the senses: taste, touch, sight, sound, smell and thinking. (in Buddhist philosophy, thinking, or consciousness itself, is considered a sense.) There are numerous examples in Zen literature of people who were enlightened by hearing a sound, seeing a sight, being hit with a broom or reading a passage in a book. One master was even enlightened in a dream.

Al Rapaport

Chapter 6

Difficulty in the Beginning

Each of us has a unique set of karmic circumstances that influence what our particular issues or difficulties will be in meditation as in life. But rather than being stopped by the difficult issues, we can develop the inner strength to grow from adversity.

Al Rapaport

The difference between sitting still and not sitting still is deciding that no matter what, you are going to sit still. One student of mine was constantly twitching, and finally she asked, "Why can't I sit still?" My answer to her was that she hadn't yet determined to sit still. There is no lightening bolt from the sky that gives us this miraculous power, it must come from our own determination.

Many years ago I asked my first teacher, Kozan Kimura Roshi, "How long is it good to sit for?" He roared out, "You can sit until you die!" The fact is, our ability to sit still is far greater than we usually give ourselves credit for. Breaking through our perceived limits and expanding our ability is an essential part of progression in meditation. Difficulty, which everyone experiences, creates internal strength, which benefits our practice and our life. Normally, we seek comfort and release from difficulty, but the fact is if we want to experience deep insight we must at times enter into the areas that are the most difficult for us to face. Each of us has a unique set of karmic circumstances that influence what our particular issues or difficulties will be in meditation as in life. But rather than being stopped by the difficult issues, we can develop the inner strength to grow from adversity.

In his youth, the Buddha was a pampered prince in a wealthy palace with every sensual pleasure available to him. When he left home on his quest he then practiced many austerities for years prior to his enlightenment under the Bodhi Tree. For awhile he practiced with yogis who lived in the forest naked consuming only leaves and grass. At one point, after fasting for some time, Gautama collapsed beside a stream, near death. A kind, young woman happened to find him there, and fed him, after which he quickly recovered. He realized, after regaining his strength, that both the path of unlimited pleasure and that of self-mortification was counterproductive. This led him to develop the teaching of the *Middle Way*. That is, not creating excess difficulty, but also not being attached to comfort. Although practitioners today have many comforts unheard of in the past, we still can find a balance that fosters our practice. This balance is different for everyone, and can change over time.

In many cases, what stops beginning meditators are the psychological/emotional barriers which arise through the self-inquiry process. This process is not designed to lead us to constant bliss at first, but rather to encounter the things that we suppress and the parts of ourself which we have not totally integrated or assimilated. By its very nature, the self-inquiry process creates difficulty for us, so we don't have to seek additional difficulty as we will encounter enough just in the course of our meditation! In reading about the masters of old, it becomes apparent that every major realization was preceded by a difficult time of intense striving or questioning.

Be certain that you are giving your first attempt at meditation a good chance. Don't give up too easily, as many do. Perhaps those who quit early on are just not ready for self-examination, and will be at a later time, or perhaps they need a different technique. There is nothing preventing us from meditating except our own attitude. And yet it is presumptuous to say "everyone should meditate" as many are not ready for the challenges such a practice entails.

Chapter 7

The Blues

We are very fortunate that for human beings there is a third, or middle way to deal with suffering, and that is to simply experience it – to become one with it.

Al Rapaport

I love listening to the blues—

I just wouldn't want to live that way

        —Carl Silver, Psychologist

What now is the Noble Truth of Suffering?

Birth is suffering; Decay is suffering; Death is suffering;

Sorrow, Lamentation, Pain, Grief and Despair is suffering;

not to get what one desires is suffering;

in short: the Five Aggregates of Existence are suffering

        —The Buddhist Bible, p.23

I's up this morning, ah, blues walking like a man,

I's up this morning, ah, blues walking like a man,

Worried blues, give me your right hand

        —Preaching Blues, Robert Johnson

When Gautama Buddha began teaching after his enlightenment, he taught what are called the Four Noble Truths. The First Noble Truth deals with the fact that suffering is an inescapable part of our human existence. Yet even when we admit the validity of this teaching, our minds constantly seek to avoid the reality before us when that reality is unpleasant. When this occurs, we suffer.

Avoiding that which is painful is rooted in an ancient way of reacting called the fight or flight syndrome. For instance, when an animal is confronted with pain or distress, its reaction is either to run from it or to turn and fight it. This behavior is obviously rooted in the desire to continue to live free of pain, which all sentient beings possess. However, on a physiological and psychological level during meditation, the fight or flight syndrome manifests as both mental and physical movement. When we are confronted with physical pain, or with uncomfortable thoughts or feelings, our first tendency is to attempt to escape by moving the body, or allowing the mind to move on to various fantasies, thoughts and desires. When this attempt fails, as it inevitably does during prolonged meditation, we resort to fighting, or resisting through mental and physical tension. But what works for an animal in a life or death struggle against an outside force doesn't work for us, because what we are really fleeing from or resisting during the meditation process is our own mind! Since our mind follows us wherever we go, it is fruitless to attempt to avoid it. Whether we realize it or not, a major point of meditation is to get us to confront and go through our own particular suffering or difficulty.

When my son was two years old, he was knocked over by a small wave at the beach. For years afterwards, he wouldn't go near the water. He was not aware at that young age that his avoidance was due to an incident from the past, but nevertheless, the unconscious message was that water was dangerous! In the same way, we all avoid this or that pain or difficulty because of our prior conditioning. In most cases we aren't aware that our choices are so conditioned by the past, and we rationalize our reluctance to take on difficult tasks with half-baked excuses. Only by freeing ourself of the past can we fully experience the present. As Sasaki Roshi, an old Japanese Zen master once said, "Pain is your friend." Without it, we can remain in delusion for a lifetime.

Our own suffering can either have a positive effect, in the sense that it leads us to a place of greater understanding, strength and enlightenment, or it can have a negative result, in that it can embitter or harden us so that we abandon compassion for ourselves and others. The difference between a strong person and a weak person is not the degree of suffering they experience, but rather that the strong person does not allow the suffering to stop him or her from continuing on with their practice. The weak person, on the other hand, uses suffering and difficulty as an excuse to give up their goal. There is not any one kind of person that is intrinsically stronger or better suited for meditation than anyone else – it's just that some are willing to continue getting on the horse after they fall off, and do it for as long as it takes.

We are very fortunate that for human beings there is a third, or middle way to deal with suffering, and that is to simply experience it – to become one with it. Not avoiding, not resisting, just totally experiencing the totality of our suffering is a very difficult thing for most of us to do. The old blues singers knew this truth: when you feel the blues totally, and sing from that place of feeling, it somehow makes it better. After awhile, we realize that it is the avoidance of suffering itself that prolongs the agony. If we can learn to consciously immerse ourselves in our suffering when it occurs, while not losing track of what we are doing, we can learn amazing lessons from it. In addition, by not avoiding suffering we tend to get through it quicker, and can devote more of our energy to other things.

> *Worked all the summer, and worked all the*
>
> *fall,*
>
> *I had to take my Christmas, in my overall,*
>
> *But now she gone, and I don't worry,*
>
> *Because I'm sitting on top of the world.*
>
> *–Blues Artist, Howlin' Wolf*

Al Rapaport

Chapter 8

The Sport of Sitting Still

We have to feel our meditation in the very marrow of our bones and let it permeate our entire body and mind simultaneously.

Al Rapaport

In Zen we say that body and mind are not separate. You have to get your mind and body working together to experience what meditation is about. For instance, say we want to learn karate. We could read twenty books on martial arts and understand them all, yet still not be able to throw a punch. Understanding karate on an intellectual level may be useful in some sense, but it doesn't help us to learn the activity itself. Once our body starts performing the movements, however, it imprints or teaches the mind in a very direct manner. In a sense it's the same with meditation, in that sitting the body down and keeping it still imprints the mind with its stillness. Stillness of body always goes hand in hand with stillness of mind during meditation.

We could almost call meditation the sport of sitting still, because we have to involve the entire body in the meditation process to understand what it is about. It is a very physical activity. Just sitting and thinking without the gut-level body-feeling-experience doesn't get us anywhere. Of course, in a sense meditation is the opposite of a sport, as the point of it is to sit still and do nothing! But because this runs so counter to our usual conditioning, it is surprisingly difficult for most of us to accomplish.

This brings us back to the difference between thinking and direct feeling/experience. Direct contact with the actual sensations that arise during meditation is essential to passing beyond our fixation on the intellect. Some people take to this rather easily, but others have a hard time of it. Some are difficult to wean from their thinking addiction, perhaps because their experience of the mind is that of a thinking organ, rather than seeing it in a more holistic sense. It is very threatening to those who think they understand the mind to be faced with actual feelings in their body. This very avoidance of what is happening physiologically within us is the cause of tremendous suffering, as it enables us to skirt what the real issues are in our lives.

Any transcendence that we experience is always realized

through the body itself, although our viewpoint on what the body actually is can change radically as our insight deepens. We have to feel our meditation in the very marrow of our bones and let it permeate our entire body and mind simultaneously. This is an important key to practice.

Chapter 9

Disturbances

Sometimes, just when we think we have become somewhat expert in dealing with our monkey mind, deep disturbances rear their ugly heads, prompting us to fall into despair.

Al Rapaport

Once we cease being aggressive towards our emotions, cease trying to change them, once we experience them properly, then transmutation can take place.

The irritating quality of the emotions is transmuted once you can experience them as they are.

Transmutation does not mean that the energy quality of the emotions is eliminated; in fact it is transformed into wisdom, which is very much needed.

–Cutting Through Spiritual Materialism, Chogyam Trungpa, p.236

There's a guy I used to run into periodically on the street who had been meditating for a number of years. Once he engaged me in a discussion regarding the fact that when he maintained a regular meditation practice his mind would become very unsettled, causing him to stop meditating totally for some time. He couldn't figure out what the problem was. My response to him was that the meditation was bringing up issues and emotions that he didn't want to admit were there. It doesn't matter whether he has been meditating ten years, or ten days, if he isn't willing to face his deeper conditioning he will never get beyond it. My advice to him was to get into the disturbance and enjoy it – to learn to utilize the disturbance rather than running from it. Disturbance happens within our own minds, and as such only we can do something about it.

There are varying levels of disturbance that we encounter at different stages of our meditation. When we first start practicing, our thoughts will not stop, causing us no end of agitation. Then, after some time has passed, the initial mind activity we noticed begins to slow and disappear, but it is often replaced with deeper, gut-wrenching emotions which must be faced and resolved. Sometimes, just when we think we have become somewhat expert in dealing with our monkey mind, deep disturbances rear their ugly heads, prompting us to fall into despair. At this point it is essential to dig in and not be deterred – to own our experience through and through.

In meditation, we eventually see that what we call emotion is simply a kind of thought that has become imbedded in our bodies and minds through deep attachment. There is tremendous energy in emotion that can be harnessed, or transmuted, as Trungpa Rinpoche says above. This turns emotion from a disturbance into a way of generating energy to help ourselves and others in a positive way. It is truly amazing how powerful the energy of emotion is, and how much we can do with it when it's taken out of the conceptual matrix we usually put it in.

Of course, there are those who are not mentally stable to begin with who are sometimes not prepared to deal with the increased awareness of personal suffering which meditation can bring on. Those in this category would be advised to seek counseling and consult with a therapist who is also a meditator before getting too deeply into it. Meditation is a powerful tool that is definitely not for everyone, but we also don't want to exclude those from instruction who can benefit. When I lived at the Zen Center of Los Angeles there was a man who practiced there who constantly talked to himself. Sitting on the porch, walking down the street – whatever he was doing he was always talking to his imaginary friend. Of course, we all do this internally to a greater or lesser degree, but this was an extreme case of one who couldn't stop vocalizing his internal dialogue! But somehow, in the meditation hall, he was totally silent, and could even do a week-long silent meditation retreat. As soon as he emerged from the meditation hall the dialogue continued as if he had never stopped!

Remember, a reasonably sane person has nothing to fear from meditation except fear itself!

Chapter 10

Mind Traps

The original teachings of the great Zen masters are designed to help free us, not make us slaves to some religion or dogma.

Buddhist teachings are prescriptions given according to specific ailments, to clear away the roots of your compulsive habits and clean out your emotional views, just so you can be free and clear, naked and clean, without problems.

There is no real doctrine at all for you to chew on or squat over...

–Zen Essence, Zen Master Yuansou, p.79

Al Rapaport

It is extremely important to remember that Buddha was not a Buddhist, just as Jesus was not a Christian. Both were highly enlightened teachers who saw illness all around them, and offered a prescription, or a series of prescriptions to effect a cure. The greatest spiritual teachers of all time were not bound by what had been done before them, and were not hindered by labels or classifications. All of the rules and regulations of spiritual practice seem to be created by those who come after the death of a great master. Ignoring the basic teachings of the masters, they often create the exact situation the original teachings were designed to dispel!

It is so easy to get stuck in a particular, comfortable viewpoint. Obviously, when a disciple of a great master interprets the teaching, it is going to have a bit of a bias. Likewise, when eminent Buddhists gathered together several centuries after the death of Gautama Buddha and came up with a code of hundreds of written rules of conduct, they were reflecting more their own dogma than Guatama's teachings in many ways. In a effort to emulate a great master's teachings, disciples and followers of all sorts codify and solidify what essentially cannot be codified and solidified, namely the essence of the teaching. Thus, dogma arises from those less creative and less secure in the true teachings, which transcend dogma and codification. Master Yuansou continues:

> *If you will not believe in yourself, you pick up your baggage and go around to other people's houses looking for Zen, looking for Tao,*
>
> *looking for mysteries, looking for marvels, looking for buddhas,*
>
> *looking for Zen masters, looking for teachers.*
>
> *You think this is searching for the ultimate, and you make it into your religion,*

> *but this is like running blindly to the east to get*
> *something that is in the west."*

– *Ibid, p.79*

Evidently students in the fourteenth century had very similar weaknesses to those today. The original teachings of the great Zen masters are designed to help free us, not make us slaves to some religion or dogma. Only when we realize that the truth comes from within can we emulate the freethinking masters of old, whatever religion they inadvertently spawned. But, how can we free ourselves from the confines of our conditioning, and learn to live the life of the enlightened master? Understanding *karma*, or cause and effect, is certainly a good beginning.

Chapter 11

My Karma Ran Over My Dogma

In a way, we could say that every single action we take in this life goes on infinitely in some form or another.

Al Rapaport

...To realize the full potential of being human, we must examine the concept of karma, the process of cause and effect, especially the relationship between our actions and their results.

We need to recognize fully the unfailing connection between what we do now and what we experience later.

–The Dharma, Kalu Rinpoche, p.44

In simple terms, what does karma mean?

It means that whatever we do, with our body, speech or mind, will have a corresponding result.

Each action, even the smallest, is pregnant with its consequences. It is said by the masters that even a little poison can cause death, and even a tiny seed can become a huge tree.

–The Tibetan Book of Living and Dying, Sogyal Rinpoche, p.92

The word karma is common in our culture these days, largely because the idea of reaping what one sows is taught in many religions and philosophies. Our *karma* could be described as the result of the totality of our thoughts and actions from the past. In other words, karma is another way of describing the cause and effect relationship that exists throughout the entire universe. Not understanding how karma functions is the cause of tremendous suffering for ourselves and everyone around us. This idea, while being extremely simple, is somehow difficult to embrace, as we fear taking responsibility for the entire universe we have created.

Of course, no matter how much we meditate, we will always have some specific kind of conditioning, or karma, and will act in accordance with it. So, whatever our past conditioning is determines how we evaluate and react to an experience.

59

What makes a tremendous difference in our lives is whether we are aware of this process. Usually we don't feel that we have choice, that we are in our present state because of circumstances beyond our control. What an experienced meditator learns is that we always create our situation and that by virtue of our past karma we are where we are because of decisions we have made. These may not have been conscious decisions, but because some decisions were unconscious does not free us from responsibility for them. Obviously, being aware of what karma we are creating and how we are creating it is of supreme importance if we are to take full responsibility in our life.

Zen does not teach that we can choose everything that happens to us in life, but what we can choose is how we react to what comes up for us. In fact, whether we realize it or not, we are constantly choosing a path, constantly making our way through picking and choosing one thing over another. Much of this picking and choosing activity is unconscious, and happens in such a way that we are unaware that a choice is being made at all. Therefore, a crucial key to discovering our personal freedom is to learn to fully bring choice into the realm of the conscious mind.

Again, this is a simple idea which is easily said, but how do we actually go about doing it? Well, Zen teaching is that the medicine for lack of awareness is meditation. Turning our attention inward through mediation can make us aware of our unconscious patterns that keep us from our innate freedom of mind. Of course, with freedom comes responsibility, the dreaded word that strikes fear into the heart of many a spiritual seeker! If we are to make our choices in a fully conscious and free manner it only stands to reason that we cannot blame others when we suffer the consequences. Thus, we create our future karma through the actions which we have chosen in any given moment.

Our karma can manifest in three ways: instantly; later in our life; or in future lives. All of us have experienced instant karma at one time or another. Perhaps you have gotten angry, and kicked something, only to hurt your foot, or maybe yelled at someone and created a conflict – both are examples of very rapidly experiencing the fruit of negative action. However, many times the seeds of negative karma remain buried until a later date – and at times those who have created evil suffer the consequences while going through the dying process itself. But in a way it is even more important to see how evil deeds from a previous existence can manifest in future lives. This explains why certain seemingly blameless people, or those living exemplary lives, can have terrible things befall them. Rather than simply being caused by the arbitrary actions of a wrathful god, in Buddhism these events are seen as the playing out of karma created throughout many lifetimes.

Buddhist teaching is that everything that exists now has a basis in, or is a result of, past karma. In other words, nothing happens independent of its causes, and everything happening now has a result. In a way, we could say that every single action we take in this life goes on infinitely in some form or another. Again, this view points us to the supreme importance of personal responsibility in our lives and actions. It's not simply that a patriarchal god up in the sky will judge us, it's that our negative actions reverberate on and on, as do our positive ones. It's our choice – that's the wonderful thing, but also the terrible thing. There isn't anyone else to blame.

Al Rapaport

Chapter 12

Freedom & Perfection

To truly experience freedom, we have to be able to see things from both the relative and the absolute perspective and not get stuck in either one.

Al Rapaport

A monk once asked Master Kempo,

"The Bhagavats of the ten directions have one way to Nirvana. I wonder what this one way is."

Kempo held up his stick, drew a line, and said, "Here it is!"

–Mumonkan, Case 48

What is freedom, and can human beings really experience it? How can we say that the world is perfect as it is when it often appears to be the opposite? To gain an understanding of Zen teaching on this point, we need to see that there are two ways of looking at this issue. One is the *relative side*, which is that the world is never going to be perfect, that there will always be problems. But then there is also what we in Zen practice call the *absolute* side, which is that from the perspective of wholeness or oneness the entire universe is perfect the way it is, suffering and all. For someone who has achieved this perspective, the earth with all its imperfection is the enlightened Buddha-mindfield. So, whether this earth is a minefield or a Buddha-mindfield depends on how we experience it.

To truly experience freedom, we have to be able to see things from both the relative and the absolute perspective and not get stuck in either one. To be attached to the relative level means that we believe that just a little more money, a little larger SUV, a little larger house or a little better relationship will give us the freedom we need. The problem is, no matter how much we get, it just doesn't seem to do the trick. All those extra things require maintenance, and more and more of our time goes to creating and maintaining this kind of material wealth. Then we wonder why we aren't as happy as we're told by the advertising we should be!

On the other hand, if we have some kind of spiritual beyond body experience we can just as easily get so attached to it that we

65

cannot drop it to see the relative world around us when necessary. Life is not always perfect and wonderful – there is suffering, pain and destruction all around us, and we need to be able to empathize with those that are suffering in order to do any good. Sometimes life is calm and clear, and other times it is terrible and chaotic, so to be able to freely move between functioning in the relative while seeing the absolute state underlying all reality is very important to a spiritual understanding. Zen practice is about letting go of the relative self in order to realize oneness, but then after you have that experience of awakening, letting go of that so you can go on to the next stage. This is a very subtle point that many spiritual systems do not address, that it is necessary to avoid getting attached to both the relative aspect of life and the universal aspect. We have to be able to freely move between them. We need to be able to function in the relative world, to keep clean, to eat food, to relate well to others, but at the same time we need to be able to see the oneness of the entire universe. Nothing can be left out, or we are not truly free.

So, what is freedom? Well, if it was a fixed state of being of some type, it wouldn't be totally free. Zen teaching is that any fixed state is a trap sooner or later. Could it be that freedom is simply the realization that we can choose at any time, and in any situation? Doesn't this define freedom itself, that whatever happens we can choose – choose to go right or left, to do good or evil, to live or die? If we take any option off the table, whether it be ego, anger, lust, or selflessness, clarity and enlightenment, we limit our options and our freedom. We have an infinite range of tools to use in our tool chest – why not keep them all handy? In Zen training we use meditation as a way of learning how deeply our ability to choose goes.

Meditation is simply being aware of our own lives, of what we have created. We take our attention, which is normally focused outside, and turn it inward. What do we see when we turn our attention inward and start noticing our own body and mind? At first we see whatever we've created in our life, and that creation usually feels stuck in some way. We don't feel free because of conditioned patterns that keep us in certain narrow parameters of experience. The fact is that we are always free. We just need to free ourselves from the feeling that we aren't.

It's not the conditioning that makes us feel one way or the other, it's that we bind ourselves. There is a difference. In one case we are making conditioning an object and in the other case we realize it is part of us. The more we keep bringing it back to right here, to what is happening in this body and mind in this given moment, the easier it is to deal with this issue. When the conditioning is "out there" it is an amorphous thing that is unapproachable, but actually our conditioning is right in our own bodies and minds. That's why the meditation where we are observing body sensations is so excellent, because it is through the noticing of the sensations that we notice our patterns, both physiological and mental. I've never found anyone that could describe any psychological pain they were in that didn't have a physical component. We don't usually notice this. Normally, psychological pain is regarded as separate from physical, and yet upon closer examination the physical component always reveals itself. Again, body and mind are one – psychological and physical are one.

The problem is, we don't want to be responsible for our conditioning. We want to feel that "the reason I punched this guy is because he did something to me," or "the reason I'm not happy is because of my boss," or "the reason I fly off the handle is the whole world is down on me." We avoid responsibility for our actions, because if we are responsible it means we need to do something to change, and personal change is a daunting obstacle for many of us. Often we want things to change, but don't want ourselves to be a part of what actually changes.

67

Al Rapaport

Chapter 13

Deja Vu All Over Again

As our meditation practice deepens, we find that moment to moment reality is a timeless state.

Al Rapaport

From the Buddhist point of view, the main argument that 'establishes' rebirth is one based on a profound understanding of the continuity of mind.

Where does consciousness come from? It cannot arise out of nowhere. A moment of consciousness cannot be produced without the moment of consciousness that immediately preceded it.

–The Tibetan Book of Living and Dying, Sogyal Rinpoche, p.91

One of the most basic tenants of Buddhist meditative practice is belief in the existence of consciousness before birth and its continuance after death. In other words, we have all lived many times before and will continue to do so in the future. Although there were parallels to this belief in early Christian writings and in esoteric Judaism, for the most part this idea is difficult to accept for the Western-trained mind. Although we can practice meditation without this belief, it is an integral part of the teaching that we need to come to grips with at some level.

The Buddhist sense of transmigration differs from that of reincarnation, in that the term "reincarnation" implies that there is a "soul" that reincarnates. As Sogyal Rinpoche's preceding quote indicates, Buddhism teaches that there is a continuance of consciousness or mind itself, not the rebirth of a particular entity or being. This constantly changing mind, through its attachment to life, is repeatedly drawn towards rebirth in other bodies, in which the karma created by past existences is experienced. It is said that through prolonged spiritual practice, a highly realized master can actually *choose* to be reborn in a particular time and place in order to help teach others. This type of being is called a *Bodhisattva*.

Of course, in a sense we are all Bodhisattvas! In one way or another, we all choose our own path, although this may not actually be a conscious choice. Nevertheless, a choice is being

71

made at all times, including the choice of manifesting as a physical being. Realizing that this amazing journey we are all on is the reality of life is a profoundly liberating experience. Why cling anxiously to this one existence when it is but a small part of an infinite journey? Thus, the liberation of our mind is the realization of the continuation of the mind throughout all space and time. In a way, we can't even say that the Buddha-mind continues, as it is beyond distinctions of beginning, ending, continuing or stopping. Language really fails us in this, as it can't be described or categorized, only experienced.

Chapter 14

Does Anybody Really Know What Time it Is?

When our dependence upon thinking wanes, the timeless moment grows in power.

Al Rapaport

...are the effects of the timeless to be judged by the measurement of time? If we can understand what we mean by time, perhaps it may be possible for the timeless to be; but is it possible to discuss what that timeless is?...

It can never be talked about or communicated except through the means of time; but the word is not the thing, and through time the timeless obviously cannot be understood. Timelessness is a state which comes only when time is not.

−Commentaries on Living, 2nd Series,

J. Krishnamurti, p.106

There's no doubt that our modern conception of time as a fixed, immutable thing is the cause of tremendous suffering in our lives. We constantly hear the expression, "I don't have enough time", and "not having enough time" is a frequent excuse for those who really don't want to meditate.

Upon closer examination we find that time simply does not exist as the linear, sequential process we first believe it is. In fact, if we cling to this concept it is virtually impossible to meditate for long periods, as we find ourselves constantly moving and worrying about when the meditation period will end.

We certainly can't deny that the hands on a clock move, signifying a set period has elapsed, but the psychological sense of fixed time is belied by our own experience. For instance, everyone has noticed that "time passes quickly when you are having fun." Why is this? It's simply that when we are not occupied with time, i.e. enjoying the moment, we don't experience its passage in the same way. Being absorbed in the present, psychological time ceases for us. So, thought and intention govern our experience of time.

The issue of how or whether we experience time passing is very important to our meditation. It we are continually occupied with time, experience of the moment eludes us. As our meditation practice deepens, we find that moment to moment reality is a timeless state. More specifically, time and thought are integrally related. When our dependence upon thinking wanes, the timeless moment grows in power.

Being present in the timeless moment to moment reality is what Zen is all about. Only by being in this way can we relax and truly experience sounds, tastes, touch or other phenomena as they are without our self-imposed ideas and time restraints.

Time as a fixed concept is so important in today's world. But even with all the time saving machines and devices we now have in our lives, how many of us truly feel that we have more time than those of the past did? Our concept of time has doomed us to constantly attempt to create more leisure while rushing from place to place to make the money to get that leisure. It's one of the great curses of modern society that we experience constant stress because we just don't have the time to do everything in our lives. To practice Zen, we must learn to let go of the manic desire to constantly be doing something. We need to create space in our lives to meditate – space in our lives to experience reality.

Chapter 15

The Sound of One Hand
or What Good Is a Gateless Gate?

The Zen Koan points us to the fact that the big questions of life, death and our true nature simply cannot be addressed in a solely logical manner.

Al Rapaport

Open Mind Zen
A Guide to Meditation

Master Kyogen said, "It is like a man up a tree who hangs from a branch by his mouth; his hands cannot grasp a bough, his feet cannot touch the tree.

Another man comes under the tree and asks him the meaning of Bodhidharma's coming from the West.

If he does not answer, he does not meet the questioner's need. If he answers, he will lose his life. At such a time, how should he answer?"

–Koan by master Kyogen, Zen Comments on the Mumonkan p.53

The Zen Koan is certainly one of the most unique devices ever invented to stimulate spiritual awakening. Koans are often misunderstood by scholars and meditators who have not had their understanding tested by a master who has traveled that path before them. Such testing is essential, and it is a major component of Zen training, as we can fool ourselves in so many ways into thinking that our understanding of a koan is complete when it is not.

Simply put, a koan is a word, phrase or story which is designed to force one to access the state beyond thought. This does not mean that koans have no answer or that any answer will do (a common misunderstanding). On the contrary, each koan has a distinct and correct answer, although the answer can take many forms which may or may not include speaking. The point of the koan as an exercise is to wean us from our overdependence on logical, sequential thought as a means to solve all problems. A koan can only be solved by experiencing it 'holistically'. That is, we have to totally become one with the question in order to discover the answer. Our whole body and mind must come into play if we are to discover our true nature and break through the wall of conceptual thought.

In the West, and especially in modern times, we tend to view any issue that can't be solved logically as abstruse or paradoxical.

The Zen Koan points us to the fact that the big questions of life, death and our true nature simply cannot be addressed in a solely logical manner. It's not that there is anything wrong with logic, but it is too narrow to bring us to the totality of experience necessary for true understanding.

The koan which begins this chapter is often called, "Kyogen's man up a tree." It is a classic and vivid example of a story which defies a logical answer, and yet an answer is exactly what the Zen teacher demands. Bodhidharma, who according to legend brought Zen from India to China about 520 A.D. is often the focus of Zen koans. Asking why he came from west to east is akin to asking, "What is the essence of Zen," or, "What is the essence of life and death?" Indeed, it could be said that we are all hanging from the tree by our teeth – we can lose this life at any time. Only through becoming totally one with the man, tree and question does a solution to this dilemma arise.

Koans do not necessarily have to be classic Chinese Zen stories or riddles. For instance, during the Kamakura era in Japan Zen teachers had numerous samurai students who knew little or no Chinese. Thus their interviews had to be conducted with few words, and classical Chinese language was out. These teachers developed a whole system of koans which related to common themes in Japanese life and practice. In a way, the warriors made great Zen students, as they faced death on a regular basis, and they tended to take the practice very seriously.

> *Nanjio Masatomo, a master of the spear, was at Kenchoji to worship, and afterwards spoke with priest Gio about using a spear on horseback.*

> *Gio said, "Your Honor is indeed well versed in the art of the spear, but until you have known the state of wielding the spear with hands empty, you will not penetrate to the ultimate secret of the art."*

> *Nanjio said, "What do you mean?"*

> *The teacher said, "No spear in the hands, no hands on the spear."*
>
> *The spear master did not understand.*
>
> *The teacher said further, "If you don't understand, your art of the spear is a little affair of the hands alone."*
>
> *–Zen and the Ways, Leggett, p.102*

Again, here the spear master is being asked to do something that is totally impossible! How can he wield his weapon without using his hands? And yet this question points to the essential matter in life, that which is ungraspable yet must be understood. How do you eat? How do you walk? Without realizing the underlying implications, these acts are just a matter of chewing and putting one foot in front of the other. Through meditation practice, we can understand the purpose our life has.

Years ago, I did a retreat at Mount Baldy Zen Center in Southern California led by Sasaki Roshi, a famous Japanese Zen Master who has lived in the U.S. for many years. He spoke very little English, and so had to develop simple koans to communicate with his American students. When a new student came before him in interview, he would ask, "When you see a tree, how do you realize yourself?" Or, "When you hear the sound of the bird outside, how do you realize yourself." In Zen, the senses themselves are the pathways to enlightenment, but the student must become totally one with the sight or sound to understand what these koans point at. If even a small conceptual barrier exists, it creates a gap as wide as an ocean. The answer to the koan will never become clear if we cling to some conception about it.

There are hundreds of traditional koans, most of which either came from China from between 600 and 900 A.D. or from feudal era Japan. But truly, any question or issue in our life that defies logical answer can be a koan. Somehow, if we use our meditation to sit with a question that is perplexing us, openly and without conception, an answer to our dilemma will arise. We just have to let it happen, and give the meditation process time to work. The more we allow the Buddha-mind to come up with answers to the unanswerable, the easier our life becomes. Buddha-mind includes everything, so naturally it includes both the question and the answer. If we become one with the question, we realize the answer was always present – the ego just had to step aside to let it manifest.

First There Is A Mountain

Why carry around a dead self that is actually a concept rooted in non-reality?

Al Rapaport

Shunyata

There is a famous passage in the Heart Sutra, which is considered in Zen to be the seminal teaching of the Buddha on the nature of meditation practice, which states, "Form is emptiness, emptiness is form." The ancient Sanscrit word *shunyata* is translated into English as *emptiness*, but in English this word usually refers to a vacuous or nihilistic state, which is almost the opposite of the original sense of shunyata. This emptiness or no-thing-ness of shunyata is what we begin to experience when we practice meditation. It has many names: God (without the patriarchal personality), Buddha, True Nature, Buddha Mind, Unborn Mind, Big Mind, Universal Consciousness, etc. The more we investigate the mind the more we realize that everything is empty, or devoid of a fixed, solid nature. At first we believe that there is a fixed solidity to the material world, but when this concept is subject to the microscope of meditative examination we find that we are mistaken. The idea of the solidity of the material world begins to break down under observation, and we begin to experience the reality of shunyata. Even on a scientific level it has been discovered that what we perceive as solid matter is simply a field of electrons orbiting around a minute nucleus. There is very little matter in matter, but rather small particles in an electrical suspension field.

Now, if one has a really strong realization in body and mind of the fact that everything is empty, this is called an enlightenment experience, or *satori* in Sanscrit. (This experience is explained in greater depth in the next chapter, *How to Catch an Ox*). The second part of the teaching, that "Emptiness is Form," is an even more advanced stage of practice in which we let go of the experience that everything is emptiness and realize that emptiness is manifest in form, or the material world. So, the old saying, "First there is a mountain, then there is no mountain, then there is", means that first a mountain appears solid, then *empty*, then as form manifesting emptiness.

Those with deep meditation experience know that the third stage of there being a mountain again is experientially very different from the initial state. It describes a way of seeing the universe in which all forms (sounds, tastes, sights, etc.) are seen as not simply being empty, but as *expressions* of emptiness. A mountain is just a mountain, a sound just a sound. Both aspects have to be experienced in order to understand Zen. Unfortunately, many meditative systems only teach discovery of emptiness, and do not teach that remaining attached to that realization is a serious dilemma.

So, according to this teaching, everything in the universe is empty, including our self. If we can fully experience this fact it is a tremendous relief. Why carry around a dead self that is actually a concept rooted in non-reality? It takes a tremendous amount of energy to maintain the nonexistent self. There is, however, a lingering sense of self that at first defies all efforts to let go of it. No matter how many times we are told that the self is unreal, it *feels* as if there is an observer. This feeling that the observer or self exists is the root of our problem with meditation and our life. To solve this dilemma, we must go beyond our normal, intellectual way of viewing reality – go deeply into the mind/ body *feeling* of separateness. Since the body is the only way we have of *feeling* anything, we cannot overlook it in our spiritual search. Remember, mind and body are one – when we meditate we must employ everything at our disposal in our search for oneness.

It is important to see that emptiness does not negate individuality. Each particular person is completely individual and unique without having to do anything about it, and yet a powerful experience of emptiness destroys the concept of a self separate from everything around it. It's like the five fingers on a hand – each finger is totally unique and different from the others, and yet they are all connected. A finger that does not realize it is part of the hand can't function when the hand is called upon to perform a task. Likewise, if we insist on clinging to the illusion of separateness, our vital energy and ability to function in the world is hopelessly impaired. We feel that we are continually swimming against the river of life instead of letting it carry us to our goal.

This concept of emptiness is not unique to Zen. In the Bible, for instance, it is said that we are made in God's image. This image of God, which is the totality of the universe in its pre-conceptual state, *is* the realization we attain through meditation. Thus we could just as easily substitute the word *God* for *emptiness*, although both have their conceptual traps: *God* can too often bring up anthropomorphic associations, whereas *emptiness* can bring up nihilistic ones. We have to always remind ourselves that the experience is the important thing, not how we describe it.

Samadhi & Satori

There are two more Sanscrit terms which are useful to understand, mainly *samadhi* and *satori*. Classically, these words can have numerous meanings, but in Zen practice samadhi normally refers to the constantly deepening state of effortless concentration which develops from prolonged meditation. This state is often accompanied by feelings of bliss, centeredness and well being, and has many different levels of experience inherent in it. This state, however, differs from the experience of satori, which is an instantaneous awakening to one's own true nature, or we could say the true nature of the entire universe.

The various meditation methods described in Chapter Two are employed by different systems depending on whether the experience of satori is being emphasized, or the experience of samadhi. Even the two major schools of Japanese Zen have differing opinions in this regard. In the Soto School, *shikan taza*, or *just sitting* is taught, with the idea being that a gradual deepening will result in eventual insight. Conversely, the Rinzai School uses koan practice as its primary tool in an attempt to push the student to experience a radical opening, or *satori*, as soon as possible. This battle between the philosophy of gradual awakening verses instant enlightenment has been going on in Zen circles for over 1,000 years! As was mentioned in Chapter Two, both of these methods have their strong and weak points, and we should be very clear as to what these are. Ideally, we should have the experience of both shikan taza and koans in order to achieve a balanced understanding.

It seems that the determining factor when evaluating a course of practice is our own personality type. Those who love intensity or going for it are the ones that can handle the intensity of koan practice, which can result in a relatively quick experience of enlightenment. The danger in this method is twofold. Number one, the initial experience is often very shallow, and those that mistake their limited experience for total realization can seriously fool themselves if they discontinue meditation practice. Number two, it can lead to a very goal oriented attitude about spiritual practice, which may work in the short term but can hinder progress in the long run.

Those who are more the slow, steady type often identify with the gradual cultivation of awareness over time. Eschewing spiritual materialism, these practitioners see the tangible effects of meditation over the course of their lives. Eventually, this gradual opening does result in satori, but it can take many years to achieve. The advantage of this method is that when opening does occur it usually is very deep. When doing gradual practices, though, we must guard against falling into a blissful or soporific state in which the edge of true inquiry is allowed to wane. However, many long time meditators find that changing techniques or focus at various times is the best course, as one's needs vary throughout one's life. This works well provided we explore the practice we are practicing to a very deep level, and not just quickly jump from technique to technique indefinitely.

In the Open Mind Zen technique, we begin our journey with

the Zen Dialogue Method, which will be explained more in Chapter 19. This way, the student has some degree of satori or opening from the very beginning. Then koan practice or *just sitting* can proceed with some basic understanding of the nature of the journey.

Al Rapaport

Chapter 17

How to Catch an Ox

Zen teaching is that our True Nature is always a part of us, but that we can't see it for our own delusion.

Al Rapaport

I will never forget the words of my first Zen teacher, Kozan Kimura Roshi, as he was departing L.A. for Japan. During my last interview with him he said, "Now that you have started on this path you have to finish it. You must see it to the end to be satisfied with your life." Roshi's leaving was very traumatic to me, as his help had been indispensable in the first six months of my practice. At the time I wasn't certain I could find the same connection with another teacher. I subsequently discovered how right his departing statement was.

This story brings us to the *Ox herding Pictures*, a series of ten drawings and commentary on the search for enlightenment by Kuo-an shih-yuan, a Chinese Zen Master of the 12th century. These drawings are metaphorical in nature, with the Ox representing the experience of oneness, or enlightenment, and the boy or ox herd representing the searcher for truth. We'll examine the first three pictures, which are of the most importance to beginning practitioners. The first drawing is called, *Seeking the Ox:*

> *The Ox has never really gone astray, so why search for it?*
>
> *Because of his defilements he has lost sight of the Ox. Suddenly he finds himself confronted by a maze of crisscrossing roads.*
>
> *Greed for worldly gain and dread of loss spring up like searing flames, ideas of right and wrong dart out like daggers.*
>
> *–3 Pillars of Zen, Kapleau, p.314*

At this level we feel confused and mill about seeking that which we think we have lost. In many cases people doubt that the Ox exists, and ridicule those who seek it as a way of covering up their own uncertainty about the nature and meaning of life. This is a sorry state to be in, and it only leads to suffering for ourselves and others, and yet all practitioners on the Path have experienced it. Take special note of the first sentence, *The*

Ox has never really gone astray. Zen teaching is that our True Nature is always a part of us, but that we can't see it for our own delusion.

This state of confusion is somewhat ameliorated by a seeker who has experienced the state alluded to in the second Oxherding Picture, *Finding the Tracks:*

> *Through the sutras and teachings he discerns the tracks of the Ox. He has been informed that just as different-shaped golden vessels are all basically of the same gold, so each and every thing is a manifestation of the Self.*

> *But he is unable to distinguish good from evil, truth from falsity. He has not actually entered the gate, but he sees in a tentative way the tracks of the Ox.*

> *–Ibid, p.315*

This picture refers to one who has encountered the dharma, or Buddhist teaching, on an intellectual level, and has begun meditation practice, but who has not yet personally experienced the reality of the Buddha-mind. A person in this state can be encouraged by the fact that since the tracks of the Ox exist, an Ox must have made them! In other words even though he has not experienced Enlightenment, he has encountered the teaching and believes intellectually in enlightenment. Master Shih-yuan explains further with this poem:

> *Innumerable footprints has he seen in the forest and along the water's edge.*

> *Over yonder does he see the trampled grass?*

> *Even the deepest gorges of the topmost mountains can't hide this Ox's nose which reaches right to heaven.*

> *–Ibid, p.315*

Obviously, the grass had to have been trampled by something! But what is it? Enlightenment is all around us. In fact, we *are* it! It can't be hidden anywhere, as everything manifests it. Although it might take many years, the seeker can rest assured that the Ox will someday be found.

Next is the third Oxherding Picture, which refers to an extremely important event in the life of a spiritual practitioner: *First Glimpse of the Ox:*

> *If he will but listen intently to everyday sounds, he will come to realization and at that instant see the very Source.*
>
> *The six senses are no different from this true Source. In every activity the Source is manifestly present. It is analogous to the salt in water or the binder in paint.*
>
> *When the inner vision is properly focused, one comes to realize that that which is seen is identical with the true Source.*
>
> *–Ibid, p.316*

The experience of glimpsing the Ox is our first true taste of enlightenment, our first solid confirmation that the Buddha and the enlightened masters of old were not leading us astray. There is no substitute for this experience, and words cannot convey the radical shift in awareness it brings. Seeing the Ox puts us squarely on the path of the Buddha himself, and transforms our view of life and death. In Zen teaching, this understanding must be continually clarified and deepened as time goes on.

In some Buddhist traditions, this experience is called, *entering the stream.* In a way, it might be more accurate to say that this is the experience of getting wet in the Buddha-mind-stream. This stream is the unborn mind-state that exists previous to birth and after death, and is the source of our entire existence.

However, the depth of our immersion in this stream varies greatly from person to person, and it is extremely important for one who feels they have seen the ox to seek out a genuine teacher to have the experience confirmed. I've met numerous practitioners throughout the years who were totally convinced their enlightenment was an extremely deep one, but by traditional zen standards this was not the case. The ego is a great trickster, and it is easy to be fooled.

Chapter 18

Peace and Setting the Mind

The fact is that the search lasts for as long as we believe we are lacking something, something that a teacher or a teaching can supply us.

Al Rapaport

Everyone appears to be searching for peace of mind. Case 41 of the Gateless Barrier addresses this issue directly:

> *Bodhidharma sat in zazen facing the wall. The Second Patriarch, who had been standing in the snow, cut off his arm and said, "Your disciple's mind is not yet at peace. I beg you, my teacher, please give it peace." Bodhidharma said, "Bring the mind to me, and I will set it at rest." The Second Patriarch said, "I have searched for the mind, and it is finally unattainable." Bodhidharma said, "I have thoroughly set it at rest for you."*
>
> *– Mumonkan, Shibayama, page 285*

In this koan we can see that no matter how serious of a search we are engaged in, no amount of exertion will bring us peace of mind. Even cutting off our arm to show how strong of a student we are just creates more suffering. The problem is that the controlling ego is always looking for something outside itself to solve its problems and give it peace, when the very issue is the search itself, not the fact that something is missing. In fact, the ego is biologically programmed to continually seek more, better, bigger, faster or whatever. This very drive to continue to make things better or easier is an integral part of what it means to be alive, and yet at the same time this tendency can be our own worst enemy. This is because if we allow ourselves to be constantly distracted from the present moment then we never totally experience any moment we are actually in. At the end of the day this results in a feeling that we are not satisfied with our life, which leads to wanting more of everything to fix it. A bigger house, new relationship, more money or more toys are seen as the pathway to happiness and satisfaction, and yet when we get what we want we just end up getting tired of it and wanting something else. This cycle never ends and never results in attaining peace of mind for any length of time.

In his book, *Stumbling on Happiness*, Harvard Psychology

Professor Daniel Gilbert cites the fact that Americans who earn $50,000 per year are happier than those who make $10,000 per year, but that Americans that make $5 million per year are not much happier than those who make $100,000 per year. (Gilbert, page 217) In other words, there are objective studies that indicate that past a certain point of basic comfort; we are wasting out time by devoting our life to accumulation of vast amounts of money or property. A substantial amount of our societal conditioning and certainly a lot of advertising leads us to believe that more accumulation equals more happiness, but when you look around at the rich and famous they don't appear to be in bliss. More houses, toys and money simply require more maintenance, and those who make lots of money normally spend a huge amount of their life dealing with possessions in one form or another.

Paradoxically, what brings someone to Zen practice in the first place is the very search that we are told is counterproductive! On an experiential level, we must search at first. The Second Patriarch had supposedly extensively studied Mahayana and Theravada techniques for many years, and was already middle aged when the incident cited in the koan happened. And yet, his searching had not ended – he still felt on some level that he needed something from outside of himself. It seems that we all go through this search, looking for peace this place or that, looking for satisfaction in Florida, Costa Rica, Europe or India. Or perhaps we take training after training and workshop after workshop, looking to add that little bit to our knowledge that will give our mind rest. We consult psychics, shamans, roshis, lamas, tulkus and saints hoping they will impart some "secret" method or knowledge to us that will give us what we think we need. We hungrily seek miraculous cures, healers with psychic powers and teachers with magical powers so that we feel special and good about what we are doing. Unfortunately, no matter how many certificates we earn and no matter how much money we spend, this is a recipe for constant wandering in the world of suffering.

The antidote to the suffering of the search can only come through our own practice and experience, and usually after years of the search itself. Although the guidance of a teacher or spiritual practice of some sort is usually an essential prerequisite to ending the search, in some cases they can actually prolong it. This prolonging often comes because when a student discovers that they are totally free of the need to search then they are truly independent. This is a threat to the power base and money stream that many teachers and religions enjoy, and so they continue to develop more and more hurdles a student needs to jump over to succeed. These hurdles give one a sense of accomplishment but at the same time can lead to more and more search, and hence more and more suffering.

Therefore, the search itself can become a trap, and there are a number of koans and other Zen teachings that point to this fact. At what point is the search productive for us, and at what point does it cease to be so? The fact is that the search lasts for as long as we believe we are lacking something, something that a teacher or a teaching can supply us. Even when the teaching itself is very specific about the fact that it does not provide us anything we don't already have, on some level we really don't believe it. In a way we could say that this is the mind state of the student seeker.

What turns a student into a teacher is when the student has exhausted the search – has pursued it to its depths and finally, without a doubt, can find nothing to add to the self to make it right. At that point, if total acceptance can finally be allowed to manifest, the realization dawns that "I am the Master," or, "I am the Buddha, or the Awakened One." This is true awakening - awakening to the fact that there is nothing to search for – never was and never will be. This is the most basic tenant of Zen - that there is nothing to seek and nothing to find at the end of our search.

Al Rapaport

Chapter 19

Teachers

Since the true master is reflecting spirit, and spirit is not logical, then how can we expect the teacher's actions to always meet our logical expectations?

Al Rapaport

The following statement by Carlos Castaneda's legendary teacher don Juan is an extremely clear perspective on the function of a true teacher. Just substitute *enlightened teacher* for *nagual:*

> *"You may believe whatever you want," don Juan replied undauntedly, "The fact remains, there is no game without the nagual. I know this and I say so. And so did all the naguals who preceded me. But they didn't say if from the standpoint of self-importance, and neither do I.*
>
> *To say there is no path without the nagual is to refer totally to the fact that the man, the nagual, is a nagual because he can reflect the abstract, the spirit, better than others. But that's all.*
>
> *Our link is with the spirit itself and only incidentally with the man who brings us its message."*
>
> *–The Art of Dreaming, Carlos Castaneda, p.11*

We always want our teachers to be logical, moral, and fitting the ideas we have developed of how they *should* act. But saddling the teacher with our concepts of how they should act belies the main thing we are looking for in our interaction with them. That is, how well does our teacher reflect the enlightened, or universal mind in our interactions with them. All other considerations should be secondary to the serious spiritual seeker.

At first we desire our interaction with the teacher to be comfortable, beneficial, wonderful, clean and hygienic.

When a teacher doesn't meet this expectation, one of two things happens: either we get disillusioned and leave, or we stay in the situation and eventually drop our concepts of what the teacher is and what spiritual teaching is truly about. By dropping our concepts we become much broader and deeper, and yet we still may not be able to justify the actions of that particular person logically. Since the true master is reflecting spirit, and spirit is not logical, then how can we expect the teacher's actions to always meet our logical expectations? Then again, we are always free to leave, free to vote with our feet and escape the situation we find ourselves in. In fact, we shouldn't waste our time in a community or group with which we are not happy, and certainly shouldn't remain in an abusive one. It is much better to leave altogether and be clear about the decision then to stay and constantly complain.

A key issue as to what we allow ourselves to go through with a given teacher is whether we believe that person is truly enlightened. If they are not truly enlightened, than it won't take long for us to be dragged down into whatever delusion is being put forward as the one true way. But if the teacher is truly enlightened, then by resisting his or her teaching methods we may be passing up a wonderful opportunity for spiritual growth. Referring back to Don Juan's admonition, what is crucial is that the teacher not be coming from a position of self-importance. In other words, is the teacher creating a personality cult to expand his or her own power and prestige, or to gain wealth from students? If so, it's best to leave while we can. On the other hand, we may not get another chance to encounter the true teachings in this lifetime, so we need to take advantage of the situation when it arises if the teacher is genuine.

Naturally, this leads to the issue of how we determine whether or not someone is enlightened. Unfortunately, there is no way to logically, definitively answer this question. A few years ago, a member of the meditation group I led asked me several times to go hear a particular traveling teacher who was speaking locally. "I'd like your opinion," he said, "of whether or not he is enlightened." My answer to him was that he had to look to his own feelings and intuition to justify following or rejecting that teacher's path, and that my opinion was my own and shouldn't be relied upon. That said, it certainly helps to check into who your prospective teacher has studied with and what lineage or tradition he or she comes from. With self taught masters there is no telling what you are getting. This is especially true of those who claim to have only studied with disembodied spirits, angels or ascended masters of some sort. As Sogyal Rinpoche says: "Choosing a teacher who fits our conceptual matrix is much like trying to choose who we fall in love with." It just doesn't work! Here you have to rely on and trust your deepest intuitions – your connection to spirit in order to make the correct decision. Remember that meeting a true teacher you have a deep, karmic connection with is a lot like falling in love – when it happens there is no question in your mind about the validity of the experience. But if you don't have this powerful of a hit, work with who seems the best for you at the time, with the idea that you can always change or add teacher affiliations if you need to. In ancient times many students who became great masters themselves traveled extensively to encounter various masters' teachings. It is unfortunate, in my view, that many spiritual practitioners today get totally hooked on one teachers' way, and do not investigate others to round out their training. This often results in the guru-worship syndrome wherein the student gives up all personal power and sound judgment and looks to one teacher to solve all his or her problems.

An ancient Hindu proverb states that when the student is ready the guru (or teacher) will appear. This is so because on the deepest level our inner and outer teachers are one. So, in a sense, when we are truly ready to receive the information of our inner wisdom, a physical manifestation of this wisdom appears as another person. It is extremely important that we encounter an actual physical embodiment of our inner teacher in human form. Visionary experiences can be very powerful, but when distorted by ego we can be led off on all kinds of unproductive tangents.

In Zen, teaching is accomplished through what is called the *mind-to-mind transmission*. This transmission can only occur when our Buddha-mind recognizes the Buddha-mind of our teacher – then true teaching can occur. Whether we see it or not, our Buddha-mind is always functioning – we just need to recognize that fact. A true teacher reflects our Buddha-mind back to us. As such the role of the teacher is of extreme importance to someone truly on the path.

Chapter 20

Zen Made Easy

Westerners tend to be individualists. Our egos are highly developed, and we don't take well to being beat up by spiritual practices.

Al Rapaport

> *You each received one thing from your mother when*
> *you were born – the unborn Buddha-mind. Nothing*
> *else.*
>
> *Rather than try to become a Buddha, when you*
> *just stay constantly in the unborn mind, sleeping in*
> *it when you sleep, up and about in it when you're*
> *awake, you're a living Buddha in your everyday life*
> *– at all times...*
>
> *Instead of trying to become a Buddha, then, a much*
> *easier and shorter way is just to be a Buddha.*
>
> *–Master Bankei, The Unborn, Waddell, p.50*

Zen is very simple. In fact, it is so simple that our thinking minds have trouble understanding what Zen is pointing towards. We live in a complex world, and our lives tend to be very complex as a result of our desire to have more than we already have. Zen is an excellent antidote to the complexity of life, as it constantly takes us back to the source which is untainted by our desires and aspirations. The source always exists and always will exist, and as such is always accessible to us.

Master Bankei lived in Japan from 1622 to 1693, and his teaching of the *unborn* distinguished him from other Japanese masters that had come before. He taught anybody who wanted to hear what he had to say, much as Gautama Buddha did over 2000 years before. In 1690 he led a retreat at a temple that had been built for him named Ryumon-ji in his native Hamada. It was unlike any retreat that had happened before in Japan (or since) in that thousands of people attended, both monks and lay people, men and women. In Japan at that time, there was no mixing of the sexes, or mixing of lay and priest in this manner during a practice session. Many priests and nuns from the different sects of Zen and other forms of Buddhism were in attendance (almost 1700 by some accounts), as were thousands of lay people. Such was the power of Master Bankei's teaching of the unborn mind.

His teaching was done in the common Japanese language, rather than the classical Chinese, so that anyone with a mind to listen could understand.

The Unborn Buddha Mind is always present. However, our fixation on the ego prevents us from experiencing that fact in most instances. Traditional spiritual practices from the East tend to view the ego as an adversary. In order to foster an experience of Unborn Mind, the ego is exhausted through lack of sleep, meditated to death, and/or bored to death with years of repetition of mantras, prostrations or other tasks. But there is another way to deal with the ego, which is to ask its permission to get out of the way for awhile. This is accomplished by showing the ego (or controller as we call it in this instance) how it is in its own best interest to step aside to allow the Unborn mind through. We call this technique Zen Dialogue.

Westerners tend to be individualists. Our egos are highly developed, and we don't take well to being beat up by spiritual practices. The Zen Dialogue method works with the ego rather than opposing it, validating the various parts of the self while clearly demonstrating the existence of the Unborn mind. Using this technique, someone totally unfamiliar with Zen can have an experience of the Unborn within the first hour.

Zen Dialogue is fun, and it is easy. The facilitator begins the process by asking to speak with our controller. The *controller* is that part of us, normally described as the ego, which controls which voices, or behaviors, we are manifesting at any given time. Eventually the facilitator gets the controller to see how it is in its own best interest to allow the Unborn Mind, or Big Mind, to speak. Once the participant is speaking from Big Mind, the voice of enlightenment, which we all possess, can inform the ego of its existence and scope. The controller is always trying to understand Big Mind intellectually, but obviously that's impossible. However, when it sees that it doesn't have to understand, then a kind of letting go occurs, and Big Mind can speak clearly and spontaneously.

This method, originally synthesized from voice dialogue, a technique developed by psychotherapists Hal and Sidra Stone in the 1970's, is nothing short of miraculous in its effect. Virtually everyone experiences an opening of some sort during the Zen Dialogue Process, yet this does not negate the need to practice meditation. In fact, it shows graphically how important sitting meditation is to deepen and clarify one's initial experience. Coming from someone who practiced intensively for years to answer my first koan, it never ceases to amaze me that a person unfamiliar with Zen can participate in this process and be answering koans within a few hours. This can be very disconcerting to hard core Zen people who have struggled and suffered mightily, but the fact is that all the great masters say we are walking the path whether we realize it or not! We can say that a lot of suffering builds character, and that may be true, but doesn't life throw us enough anyway? Why pile more on if we don't need to? The idea that Zen has to be difficult is based on the entrenched opposition of the ego. Once that opposition evaporates, the difficulty disappears.

In leading workshops in Zen Dialogue, I've found it very interesting that those who have the most trouble with the technique are often Zen or other meditation practitioners with extensive experience. When one has suffered for over a decade with long hours of painful sitting, the idea that we struggled for nothing is often hard to accept. But each of us goes through what we need to go through – our suffering is never for nothing provided we learn to let go of it and continue on.

> *You may think when I tell you to live in the Buddha-mind that it is lightweight, but believe me, it's just because it has such weight that you are unable to do it.*
>
> *This, however, might give you the idea that living in*

the Buddha-mind is very difficult business.

But isn't it true that if you listen carefully to my teaching, understand it well, and live in the Buddha-mind, then simply and easily, without doing any hard work, you're a living Buddha this very day.

–Master Bankei, Ibid, p.63—64

Chapter 21

The Path

It is a great challenge for us to let go of what we think is some great enlightenment and descend again into the depths of doubt.

Al Rapaport

My first experiences with meditation began when I was 17 and still a junior in high school. Through a few yoga books at the library, I began experimenting with yoga and yoga-inspired meditation. I immediately started having very powerful and vivid experiences while meditating that served to confirm that somehow I was on the right path. Many thoughts and experiences from my youth seemed to be clarified and confirmed as I practiced the techniques from those library books. It was my first taste of the benefits that regular sitting practice could bring.

Several years later I met Kozan Kimura Roshi on a trip to Los Angeles, during a time when I was not consciously looking for a teacher. My friend Shinzen Young, a Buddhist priest who is now a well known teacher himself, asked if I wanted to meet the Zen teacher he was studying with. Feeling in an open mood, I went with him to a small house in West Central Los Angeles where Kozan Roshi taught a select group of students in meditation. He spoke very little English, and so most of our communication was done through a Japanese student of his named Masako, who served as his attendant and translator. Kozan (which means *Tiger Mountain*) Roshi had an amazingly powerful presence, and everything about him convinced me that I had found a teacher. It was exactly as Sogyal Rinpoche said, like falling in love in a sense.

Not long after, I moved back to the Los Angeles area to study with Kozan Roshi, and did numerous week-long meditation retreats, or sesshins, with him and his small group. I'll never forget my first sesshin! By the second day I was in the most excruciating pain I had ever experienced, but I persevered, determined not to fail. The next day, I was gazing at a flower outside during a break period and for an instant my consciousness merged with the plant. This took me totally by surprise, and I got very excited, but the experience didn't last, and doubt soon returned. Driving home at the end of the seventh day, I was amazed at how relaxed and clear I felt – I knew I'd found the practice for me.

Kozan Roshi only remained in Los Angeles about six months longer, and when he finally left I felt a tremendous sense of loss in my life. Shinzen came to the rescue again, suggesting that I visit the Zen Center of Los Angeles, led by Maezumi Roshi. I subsequently moved to ZCLA and spent five years living and studying with Roshi and several of his assistant teachers, including Genpo Sensei (now Genpo Merzel Roshi).

I continued working with Genpo Sensei on the koan 'Mu', which I had begun with Kozan Roshi. For several years I went through the gut-wrenching experience of repeatedly coming before the teacher not knowing how to answer. After many week-long retreats, I finally reached a point where 'Mu' was before me at all times. My entire life, both awake and asleep, had Mu at its center, and I was determined not to let up for a moment until I solved the riddle.

Then, on the fifth day of a retreat, more than two years after I began work on Mu, while waiting in line for an interview with Sensei, something within me broke open and the separation between my self and the koan disappeared. I cried intensely for what seemed like hours, knowing that my life would never be the same. Sensei confirmed the experience, and I spent the next few days soaring high, reveling in my new found openness and bliss, all doubt about my Buddha nature gone.

Those who have had the experience I've just described know that doubt inevitably does return, and the incompleteness of my realization eventually became apparent, regardless of my efforts to cling to it. As the Buddha taught, we must release our attachments to everything, *especially* our enlightenments! This is a hard lesson to learn, and it took me many more years and a lot of suffering to truly understand the wisdom of this teaching.

About six years after my initial awakening, I had since left ZCLA, and lived in the countryside of Western Massachusetts. I continued to meditate on my own every morning, but wasn't really involved full time with a Zen teacher or community. Nevertheless, I continued to explore the doubt which had emerged years before, and soon discovered that Genpo Sensei had also left Los Angeles and had established Kanzeon Sangha International in Bar Harbour, Maine. Intuitively, I knew it was time to reconnect with Sensei, and on the first morning of a seven day retreat, as I sat down on my cushion, I was shocked as my whole body and mind dropped away, and my previous doubts disappeared. It was as if a great shell surrounding me had cracked open, and I emerged for the first time to see reality as it truly was. The effects of this experience were very profound in my life, and shortly afterwards, I started a regular meditation group in the nearby town of Northampton, Massachusetts. I ran the Northampton Zen Group for 12 years, and during that time taught meditation to hundreds of students.

Zen teaching emphasizes that it is essential not to get stuck anywhere, no matter how profound of an awakening we believe we have had. It is a great challenge for us to let go of what we think is some great enlightenment and descend again into the depths of doubt. I was certainly no exception to this rule. In 1993, I started traveling to Salt Lake City, where Genpo Sensei had moved, to continue my studies with him. I did several retreats, including two month-long ones, and began to feel that if I really wanted to re-immerse myself in Zen studies I would have to move close to my teacher. It was an extremely difficult decision to leave the Northampton Zen Group that I had founded, as I had many good friends there, and they depended upon me for support. But doubt in the clarity of my understanding was drawing me back to my teacher, and I couldn't let my comfortable life in Northampton stand in the way.

So, my wife and son agreed to move to Salt Lake City, and we went through the arduous process of transferring our household 2000 miles to the West. Thus began the third major phase of my Zen study with Genpo, who had now become Genpo Roshi, Roshi being the honorific title given to a Zen master.

My experience, and that of others I had seen come to Kanzeon Sangha in Salt Lake City, is that it is very difficult to just be a student – especially if you've been a teacher for awhile. Letting go of the teaching role for several years was exactly what I needed to resolve the doubt that continued to afflict me at the time. After many more koans, several more major openings and more years of sitting, Roshi saw fit to give me Hoshi, and I became an assistant teacher, giving talks and interviews at the Zen Center.

During this time, I also began the *Buddhism in America Conference.* Our first event was in Boston in January of 1997. My idea was to bring together Buddhist teachers from all major meditative traditions in America to teach together at one conference over a three-day period. I have to say that it was difficult to convince many teachers that this would be a valuable thing to do. Some well known teachers, who will remain nameless, frankly dismissed the idea, not believing it had any value. Luckily for me, about 40 teachers and 800 attendees felt otherwise, and the conference was an amazing success. Hundreds of people that had been practicing for ten or twenty years came out of the woodwork to network together at this amazing event. To my knowledge, this was the largest conference of its type ever in the Western World. Although I've produced three more Buddhism in America conferences since then (one with Naropa Institute in 2000, and with *Tricycle: The Buddhist Review* in 2001), none had the excitement and participation of that first one.

In summer of 2002, I founded Open Mind Zen in Melbourne, Florida, dedicated to the propagation of Zen teaching in a lay format, by lay teachers. After 40 years of meditation practice I can honestly say that I'm just beginning to learn what this infinitely deep practice is about. I feel extremely fortunate to have received the teaching from many masters in the past, and have dedicated my life to continuing in their footsteps to the best of my ability.

From the beginning of the formation of Open Mind Zen, my desire was to commit myself to presenting Zen teaching in a way that the average person with a job and relationships could actually progress in. This meant that some changes had to be made to the monastic model, which is really only available to those who can spend considerable time in an isolated, monastic setting. Retreats are essential, but most practitioners cannot get away for huge amounts of time because of work and family commitments. So, we are working within those constraints so that a householder does not have to feel that their practice is somehow inferior to that of a monk in a monastery.

After over five years of experimentation, Open Mind Zen is most definitely a success! We now have a new Zen Teacher, Rick Owen, and a new Assistant Teacher, Betsy Smith. Our community, made up of mainly professionals or retired professionals in their 40's, 50's and 60's, seems free of many of the "strange vibes" I've experienced in other Zen communities in the past. Perhaps it is because of the maturity of the practitioners, but I would also like to think that the sanity of our way of approaching modern Zen practice has something to do with it.

Al Rapaport

Chapter 22

How to Meditate

It is said that the mind of the past is ungraspable, the mind of the present is ungraspable and the mind of the future is ungraspable.

Al Rapaport

All you really need to meditate is the small, 3' x 3' piece of ground beneath you. Then you sit down on a cushion with your legs crossed, or in a chair if you need to, close your eyes, turn your attention inward, and voila, you are now practicing the ancient practice of Zen! It's really that simple. But a few easy guidelines are helpful when dealing with body, breath and mind.

Body (Posture)

The foundation of Zen meditation is the posture, and this is true for several reasons. First, if we are not sitting straight, we are unable to meditate without discomfort for any length of time. Second, it is difficult to get a full, complete and effortless breath when the diaphragmatic muscle below the sternum is not slightly stretched as it is when we are fully erect. My first teacher used to say that the mind moved along the spine, and so keeping it straight allows the mind's energy to travel more easily.

So, we begin from the bottom up with our legs. If we are able to sit cross-legged on the floor, the posture is made easier through the use of a *zafu*. The zafu is a round, firm cushion stuffed with either kapok or buckwheat hulls. They can be ordered through a variety of sources and also found at some health food or similar stores in various sizes. In addition, many often use a *zabuton* which is a flat, square cushion which goes underneath the zafu and provides more padding for the knees and legs. These cushion designs come to us via Japanese monasteries, where they have been used for hundreds of years. Be aware that virtually all monasteries or Zen groups in the U.S. and Europe use black zafus, the traditional color, so if you do order one that you'll be carrying around, you may want to stick with black. Actually, if you're meditating at home you can use any combination of cushions that work for you. But the zafu and zabuton, if kept out where we can see them, serve as a reminder to take the Buddha's seat on a regular basis and encourage our practice.

The zafu will help elevate your rear end, making it easier to

125

attain the rest of the posture. As far as your legs go, if you can sit in a full or half lotus, they are the most stable positions. Few Westerners I've seen can sit for any length of time in full lotus – most start out with some variation of cross-legged, and progess eventually to a half lotus. If you have knee trouble, don't even start on the floor, but use a chair that you can sit up upright in. If you do sit on the ground, the object is to form a tripod with your knees and your rear for the utmost in stability. If you have a problem sitting on the floor, using a chair is fine. Just sit forward so you can maintain the correct back position.

The next step is to be sure that you have a natural curve to your lower back – specifically, that this curve is not lost by collapsing backwards. To attain this position it may feel at first that you are pushing from the lower back, and slightly distending your lower abdominal area. If you begin to lose that curve at some point during your meditation, simply push it back into place. Eventually you will develop strength in your lower back and abdomen and this will become effortless. If the curve isn't there, the rest of the spine above the foundation will begin to sag also, resulting in discomfort and listless meditation.

The shoulders should be directly above the hips, and the head balanced on the neck and shoulders. The feeling should be that there is a line attached to the back of the head pulling upwards. This will slightly stretch the neck up. Eyes should be at a 45 degree angle looking down at the floor, and the tongue settled on the roof of the mouth, barely touching the back of your top row of teeth.

In the Zen school we use a specific *mudra* (an ancient, Sanscrit word for a particular hand position). That is, the right hand in our lap with the palm turned upward, the left on top, and the thumbs forming a bridge which creates an oval. This is called the Cosmic Mudra. It seems difficult at first, but with a little practice it becomes quite comfortable, and also helps put the weight of the arms and hands in the center of the body which promotes added balance while sitting. If you're really opposed to this position, there's no problem with putting the hands on the knees, or however you are comfortable.

Now comes the hard part...relax! Actually, if you are in the correct position, with some practice you will find that it is very comfortable.

Breath

The disposition of the breath is an incredibly important factor when practicing Zen. When the body is not sitting well and the breath is agitated, the mind is unsettled also. So ideally we want to be breathing smoothly and effortlessly, which allows the breath to become lighter as our sitting deepens. Since the purpose of the breath is to supply oxygen to the body, as we sit more still our requirement for oxygen becomes much less. As a result, the breath will become gentler while continuing to move throughout the lungs. If possible keep your mouth closed and breathe through your nose while inhaling and exhaling. Your breathing should be as quiet as possible

We accomplish this by at first focusing on the hara. This is a Japanese word indicating the area about two fingers' width below the navel. This area, thought to be the center of our being in Chinese Taoist philosophy, is the source of tremendous energy. The feeling is as if our breath is being poured into us from the top, which fills us up from the bottom.

> *Zazen (zen meditation) has clearly demonstrated that with the mind's eye centered in the hara the proliferation of random ideas is diminished and the attainment of one-pointedness accelerated.*
>
> *...Thus, one who functions from his hara is not easily disturbed.*
>
> *—3 Pillars of Zen, Kapleau, p.15—16*

127

It's a good idea to take a few very deep breaths when you first begin meditation – it aids relaxation and oxygenates the blood.

You will probably notice very quickly how integrally linked the body, breath and mind are. When our mind is extremely active, the breath usually comes in quicker, shorter gasps. Learning to relax this tightening reflex has profound implications for stress reduction and for helping calm and center the mind.

Mind

The big issue facing most beginning meditators is what to do with our mind. In fact, in the beginning most Zen teachers prescribe the same type of practice as used by others Buddhist meditation systems, namely counting the breath or following the breath. In Open Mind Zen we generally start people off by counting the inhalations, or one can count "one" on the inhalation and "two" on the exhalation. You count to ten and then start over again. However, I've used this exercise to count to 100 as a way of testing my focus, especially during retreats. If you mess up and forget where you're at, you go back to one again. A variation on this technique is to "follow" the breath, or just be aware of the inhale and exhale on a subtler and subtler level.

The greatest danger in learning to meditate is in thinking that we must somehow stop thinking in order to be meditating effectively. One of the natural functions of the mind is thinking, and although we certainly can slow the process the deeper we go in meditation, it is not necessary to stop thought to be doing valuable meditation.

It is said that the mind of the past is ungraspable, the mind of the present is ungraspable and the mind of the future is ungraspable. Since the ego's function is to grasp or accumulate as much as possible, it treats the process of meditation the same way. Because the mind can't be stopped or grasped, frustration and conflict can result. Many beginning meditators stop practicing when these feelings arise, thinking that it is just too difficult for them. The simple fact is that no matter how hard it tries, the ego can't logically understand the mind. It isn't set up to function in that way. The moment can only be experienced, not thought about, but thought itself arises in the moment. So, we need to find a way that works beyond the scope of the ego.

This is where the experience of Buddha-mind, or Big Mind comes in. Since Big Mind includes the ego, as well as thought and everything else in the universe, it has no problem assimilating the apparent paradox that the meditation process brings rise to. If we learn to utilize Big Mind to meditate with, we no longer have to worry about thinking, as we see that it arises out of Big Mind and subsides into it as well. A spacious, relaxed quality results from this understanding. As we said before, early Buddhists from the Theravadan school in India called someone that experienced Big Mind a *stream enterer*. In other words, the moment can't be grasped, but it can be experienced as a stream or river which is continually flowing. The moment we experience that the river is a reality by touching our toe into it, our life is changed forever. Zen practice is oriented towards guiding us to this experience, and then teaching us to get more and more wet in that river until we're simply floating with it. We can spend our lives resisting the flow – it is possible to go against it for awhile, but why create more suffering for ourselves and others in this way?

When we experience the stream as reality, and dive into its depths, our life then begins to flow with it instead of against it. When Big Mind is firmly experienced, the ego takes its proper place as the protector and organizer of the self, as a part of us that doesn't need to be subjugated or outwitted. In Open Mind Zen we don't oppose the ego, we work with it to understand the mind in a way that works with conflict.

About the Author

Al Rapaport has 40 years of meditation experience. For 13 years he was the Director of the Northampton Zen Center in Northampton, MA. He has served on the Board of Directors of the Zen Mountain Monastery and of Kanzeon Sangha International and studied Zen with Kozan Kimura Roshi, Maezumi Roshi of the Zen Center of Los Angeles and Genpo Roshi of Kanzeon Sangha International.

As President of Open Mind Productions, Al conceived of and produced the first *Buddhism in America Conference* in Boston, MA in January of 1997. This ground-breaking event brought together Buddhist teachers from many traditions in one setting. He compiled and helped edit the book *Buddhism in America: Proceedings of the First Buddhism in America Conference* with editor Brian Hotchkiss (Tuttle Publishing, 1998) shortly afterwards.

This was followed by conferences in San Diego in 1998, with Naropa Institute in Estes Park, Colorado in 2000 and with *Tricycle: The Buddhist Review* at the ill-fated World Trade Center Marriott several months before it's destruction at the hands of the 9/11/01 terrorist attack in New York City.

Currently, Al lives and teaches Open Mind Zen in Melbourne Florida. He is dedicated to making the essence of Zen available in a Western, lay format.